BETRAYED

Wounded Women Series

Betrayed

Broken

Burned

Introvert, She Wrote

Quiet & Badass

Gemini Moon Press

Lunar Wisdom

Lunar Magic (coming 2024)

BETRAYED

Stories From Women Who Transformed Their Broken Hearts Into Opportunities For Abundance And Purpose

Curated by Jenny Alberti and Tracey Brown

WOMEN WRITING INTENTIONALLY COLLECTIVE

Book Cover by Camilla Fellas Arnold

E-book ISBN: 978-1-959509-02-8
Paperback ISBN: 978-1-959509-03-5

Disclaimer and Content Warning

The publisher takes no legal responsibility for the details inside the stories of this book. The words and opinions are the authors' own, and the memories they describe are their lived experiences. Some of the stories contained within may be disturbing for some readers, as they explore themes related to alcohol consumption, domestic abuse and/or sexual trauma, eating disorders, suicide attempts, and mental health concerns. Readers are advised to seek professional or medical assistance as necessary.

CONTENTS

INTRODUCTION

O N 24TH JUNE 2022 (which as this introduction is being written, is exactly one year ago to the day), we were having a conversation regarding recent, painful betrayals we'd both experienced
when a book title came through, *Betrayed: The sister wounds that
broke our hearts, and how we turned the pain into opportunities for
growth, healing, and abundance.*

Although the title evolved slightly, it was love at first concept, with
both of us enthusiastically wanting to pursue it and turn it into
a reality. Despite the fact that we were both already CEOs of our
respective publishing houses, we knew immediately that it wasn't
meant to be a book that either of us produced alone, and that we
needed to create it together under a united publishing banner. At
this exact moment, the book you're about to read became the idea
that started an empire in the making. It expanded into an entire book
series, the founding of the *Women Writing Intentionally Collective*,
an online community, a podcast, and so many other exciting ideas
that we'll be rolling out over the coming weeks, months, and years.

For so long, society has conditioned us, as women, to be rivals, to compete, and to betray each other because doing so divides us and keeps us weak. But we knew that this book was our opportunity to be a part of a global shift towards collaboration and healing for the collective. In the tapestry of our lives, there are so many more stories than what has transpired within our own experiences of betrayal—these individual threads interweave the experiences of women and the ways in which we hurt each other.

If you've ever been afraid of being judged or criticized; felt isolated, alone, or excluded; been guilty of judging, envying, or being jealous of others; or felt unsafe, mistrustful, or insecure around others, chances are you've experienced the "sister wound" first hand.

This wound is deeply rooted in the patriarchy and the Burning Times where women were forced to choose sides—to either submit to the will of a society that divided and separated women from our collective knowledge and power, or to fight and die as a martyr for our beliefs. Those who submitted were often forced to betray their sisters, which has led to the collective trauma and fear of betrayal being passed down from generation to generation.

The truth is that when women come together in a true, genuine spirit of support, collaboration, and caring, we are unstoppable and unbreakable—and this is a threat to the patriarchal and hierarchical structure that has been prevalent throughout our society for hundreds, and thousands, of years.

But the paradigms of leadership and society are in flux and it is now time for us, as women, to start to heal the sister wounds and transform our patterns, to move away from the destructive nature of division and back towards the "it takes a village" model of the matriarchs in our lineage.

For women to step up and support each other, to drive each other to succeed, to celebrate each other's successes with genuine love and enthusiasm rather than envy and jealousy.

Amidst the external betrayals, we, as women, have also found ourselves struggling with the realization that we have betrayed ourselves. Society, with its expectations and conditioning, has subtly convinced us to compromise our authenticity, our dreams, and our worth. We have taken on the belief that we have to compete and betray not just others, but also our own values and desires. It's a betrayal that has divided us within and kept us from fully embracing our power.

It's time to reclaim our power and discover a path of authenticity, unity, and limitless possibilities. Throughout the pages that follow, we aim to explore the depths of our shared experiences, heal the wounds that bind us, and rediscover the strength that resides within our collective sisterhood.

With all our love,
Jenny Alberti & Tracey Brown
Sacramento, California
June 2023

I

THE GIFT OF LETTING GO

Linsey Joy

A True Fairytale of Losing a Sister

DEAR READER, LET ME tell you a story. But be wary: like the fairytales of Brothers Grimm, this true story has no happy end.

Once upon a time there were two sisters, as close as could be. They grew up side by side, sharing a room, clothes, friends, and hobbies. Making mud-pies and riding their imaginary horses together, it seemed as if the two could not be separated.

As they grew, they began to find their own paths and individuality as is natural. By grade school each had their own "best friends," but deep down they knew that title was secondary to the bond they held with each other. As young adulthood brought in romantic relationships, far away college campuses and more, the space between them grew, but always a thread remained that held them together: the bond of sisterhood.

As life went on, the two sisters' paths wove in and out of each other's, sometimes close and thick as thieves, sometimes on their own journeys apart. Yet they always came back to each other.

Now, Dear Reader, when we are children we often believe that our most cherished relationships will never change. On silver screens and book pages, we learn about "forever." This becomes the desire of our young, innocent hearts: that the ones we love will be with us evermore, stable and unchanging, walking through life together. Yet, some lives are not so fairytale perfect.

When they were barely in their twenties, it came to pass that the younger sister found she was unexpectedly with child. The older sister was there for her, as best she knew how, attending the birthing classes and even driving the younger sister to the hospital when it was time.

But then... things began to change.

Of course, the younger sister had to focus on her new family, which was harder than the older one knew. By and by, it came to be that both sisters moved back into the family home, as young adults finding their footing sometimes do. The younger sister brought her child, now five years old.

Eventually, she sought an apartment, met a new man, and began a relationship. During this time, the boy lived with his grandparents who helped to raise him. This was wonderful, as the grandparents and the boy became very close. It was also difficult, however, as the sister's parenting methods and relationship choices were challenged by her parents, which led to many arguments.

Here, Gentle Reader, is where most fairytales will begin to assign the roles of *Hero* and *Villain*. Our story, however, is not so simple. You see, those titles denote who is *Good* and who is *Evil*, which implies absolutes. In real life, Dear Reader, things are not so clear.

The parents and younger sister clashed over how to raise the boy, occasionally at first but then increasingly over time. Anger turned to resentment, which turned to outrage. The elder sister and other siblings were recruited to straighten the situation out, which only made things worse. The youngest sister felt ambushed. Infuriated, she left the family forever and forbade them to see her son.

But the grandchild and grandparents adored each other and, although forbidden, found ways to visit at church and school. Thus, the discord continued.

As the boy grew, so did the conflict. Weddings, holidays, and school events were all fraught with drama and heartache. The latest atrocities of the youngest sister became a regular conversation topic at family dinners. Eventually the wounds on both sides were so great that there remained no hope of reuniting the family.

The older sister was distraught. She felt deeply hurt and shaken by the rejection from her closest confidante. Powerless to understand the behavior of her once treasured companion, she withdrew further from the younger sister as the feud continued around her.

One night, the heartache was too much to take. At the boy's eighth-grade graduation, the older sister watched from afar as the younger sister enjoyed her new family. With her husband, in-laws, and children, the younger sister celebrated and laughed, intentionally ignoring the discarded family of origin nearby.

Suddenly feeling shunned and replaced, the older sister watched as a nephew whom she'd never met climbed on the lap of his aunt—but it was not her lap. A searing reflection of the younger sister's rejection, heartbreak struck her like lightning. Crushed, she ran out of the crowded school gym with tears streaming down her face. And then, something extremely painful—but also magical—happened.

She let her sister go.

For the future that the little mud pie-making girls had dreamed of was gone. They were no longer best friends, and never would be again. They would not grow old together, sharing life's laughter and woes as fabled sisters do. All that was left for the sister was a painful choice: continue in a never-ending battle, or accept the death of their relationship as it had been and try to move on. She knew that a wound that's picked at will never heal. So she silently said goodbye and wept for two days straight.

Surely, Sweet Reader, you are wondering, "How on Earth was that magical? How could experiencing the loss of such a close and beloved relationship be anything but devastating?"

Magical happenings in real life, Dear Reader, often do not look so pretty on the outside—but such is the gift of letting go. There is nothing remotely romantic about the process of healing. Acceptance, forgiveness, and sovereignty are not won with magic wands or fairy dust, but with work and passing time.

In the case of the elder sister, it took years of intentional effort to make progress. There were untold hours of contemplation, journaling, personal development books and seminars, plus energy healing, coaches, and even therapy. Countless tears were shed. If she'd had a crystal ball, she would have known to invest in the popular tissue brand of the day. But, alas, she did not. Of course, she focused on all of life's many twists and turns on her healing journey, not just on this relationship. Nonetheless, bit by bit, deep inner healing transpired.

Many years passed without a word between the sisters. The boy, who was now a young man, occasionally came round, giving rise to a new flurry of excitement and, predictably, drama. One Thanksgiving evening, the grandparents, who were older now and far more worn from the decades of stress and heartache, announced that he would be visiting from afar for his winter holiday. They would not, however, be allowed to see him as he was traveling on his mother's dime and she, again, forbade it. The family members at the table expressed their rage and disgust at such a blatant restriction.

"Horrible!"

"Unthinkably selfish!"

"Downright *evil*!" they exclaimed!

Taken aback, the elder sister listened quietly. Although she found the limitation juvenile and perhaps mean-spirited, calling the grandson's mother "evil" seemed a bit excessive. She now understood the importance of boundaries, for she had been learning the art of setting her own, and thus she recognized what her estranged sister had done. Moreover, as she pondered the situation further, she had a great revelation: *she was unbothered*. Of course, she was sad to see her family hurt and angry once again, but she had no need to pick up the fight herself. Her usual feeling of distress simply wasn't there.

The elder sister knew, since she was not a mother or grandmother herself, she could never fully comprehend their point of view or heartbreak, and for that she had compassion. Yet, because of the healing work she had done, she avoided being victimized by someone else's actions. Instead of feeling outraged, her healing journey had led her to a place of healthy detachment.

While her family continued to wage war, she maintained her power and emotional freedom from outside circumstances. And although it was hard to watch, she was able to let them all have their feelings without trying to fix anyone. Meanwhile, she was beautifully undisturbed. She became aware of the gift she had been given by letting go. Freedom from renewed heartbreak was hers.

Oh, Darling Reader, I did warn this fairytale has no happy end, but can you see a different kind of resolution? One built upon acceptance and letting go? There are still feelings of sadness and loss that surface occasionally for the elder sister. Grief heals in layers and waves and she still misses her dear companion, sometimes wondering if things might have been different, or if reconciliation might yet be possible. However, she finds comfort in the progress she has made toward healing the unhealable and in the peace she has claimed for herself.

My Dear Reader, peace and sovereignty can be yours too. What gentleness and grace are waiting for you just beyond heartbreak? Wishing you your own Gift of Letting Go.

With Love,
The Elder Sister

~ The End ~

2

TOXIC SISTERHOOD

STEPHANIE MOYER

How to Break the Generational Cycle of Competition Between Women

I ALWAYS HAD A longing for sisterhood. The type of friendships that would withstand the tests of time. Inseparable bonds formed out of admiration, care, love, and the need to support and uplift one another. I had such a longing for that type of friendship that it didn't matter when the relationships were toxic. My need to be accepted by others was so strong that I stayed in damaging relationships. It was hard to break free. I assumed everyone had issues and believed that if we loved and cared for people, we wouldn't turn our backs on them.

It had been over a year or so since I last saw my two best friends, Mary and Lucy. Although they were cousins, it wasn't always the three of us; in the beginning it was just Lucy and me. We first met at work but, like teenagers barely out of high school, Lucy and I were inseparable. Enjoying the type of sisterhood I had always longed for, we did almost everything together, until Lucy's ex-boyfriend, Sam, came back into the picture.

He was tall, handsome, charming, funny, and had all the makings of what I thought was an all-around good guy. Sam often told stories about Lucy constantly yelling at him, fighting with him physically, and accusing him of all kinds of ridiculous, nasty things. But I thought that if he was that bad then surely she wouldn't have taken him back into her life. Would she?

At that time, my friendship with Lucy started to wane. I could feel her pulling away from me, not taking my calls or calling me back. And when we were supposed to do something together, I was often met with lies and excuses. I assumed that she was distracted with her young one, and trying to juggle her current boyfriend and her baby's father, who had come back in the picture.

One night when I called her house, Sam answered the phone and told me they'd had this huge fight and that he had found out she was seeing someone else. He asked if I wanted to come over because he could use a friend. At the time, I didn't realize that all his charm was a mask for the narcissistic pathological liar he truly was. This was a lesson I had to learn the hard way. Unfortunately, he had a way of making me feel like I was the only woman in the world and I fell for his charm.

That night was the end of my friendship with Lucy and I—or so I thought. In reality, we maintained a back-and-forth toxic friendship for several more years.

Out of the Frying Pan into the Fire

Sam and I moved away, got married, and had a baby. Eventually, Sam did to me what he did to Lucy; he left me and the baby. But unfortunately for me, leaving me wasn't good enough for him and he had to take the one thing I had left in this world. My daughter. I'm not exaggerating when I tell you I had to move mountains to see her and get her back in my care. But that story is for another book, another time. After a year of struggles, I managed to get my daughter back in my care and we never saw Sam ever again.

After I finally got custody of my daughter, I returned to my hometown, and Mary and I became the best of friends. Permanent fixtures in each other's lives, we didn't go anywhere (except work) without the other, and at one point were even roommates. Mary and I even went on dates together. On reflection, I can see how unhealthy the relationship was on all levels. Even when we lived with our boyfriends, we were probably with each other more than we were with our significant others. And if I was friendly with anyone other than Mary and Lucy, it didn't go so well; they became the target of Mary's jealous remarks and extremely bitchy behavior.

Although Lucy and I were no longer close, which had put a wrinkle in the Lucy/Mary family dynamic, for the next decade the three of us had a relationship where Lucy, Mary, and I took turns being the third wheel. Jealousy, back-handed comments, competition for men, throwing each other under the bus, better clothes than the other, nicer cars, an endless list of unhealthy behaviors was the theme of our 'friendship.'

Then many years later, after my second divorce, I became caught in the middle of a jealous quarrel between the two—and that was it. I was done. Mentally, I couldn't do it any longer. If I was going to continue the path of growth I found myself on, I had to release them from my life once and for all. My life simply was no longer aligned with theirs.

It wasn't until I finally made that decision that I became free to make real connections with other women. Connections that weren't filled with drama and jealousy. Although it was time to break the generational cycle of toxic femininity, doing this wasn't easy. For a while, and sometimes to this day, I have moments of trauma-induced fear that I'm being talked about, that women pretend to like me only to make fun of me when I walk out of the room. Fear that they are plotting to destroy my life, or trying to sleep with my husband.

Sometimes, I still feel the impact of guilt and shame as well. All the trauma I caused and experienced has the ability to affect my relationships all these years later. Mary, Lucy, and I were all victims of each other. None of us came out of that friendship unscathed and better off than the other. We got the definition of 'Sisterhood' all wrong.

My Second Start

Angie and I met through her boyfriend, who was related to my second husband, and it quickly became the four of us. Like me, she was ambitious, funny, and outgoing; we had a great time together. Having just moved into a new town with my daughter and husband, Angie came into my life at the perfect moment. I didn't know anyone except my husband's family and friends and, with no female connections, I felt quite lonely. She was the missing piece in my life. We became close quickly because we both enjoyed shopping, hitting the clubs, and doing 'girly things' together.

After a couple of years of what I thought was a great friendship, she started acting weird. I began to notice things between my husband and her. Looks. Stares. Secret smiles. One evening, I came home from work to find Angie already at the house waiting for me because we had planned a girls' night out. As we drove away, she started to cry. When I asked her what was wrong, she kept mumbling something about being a horrible person, and my intuition kicked into high gear. But I ignored it!

Deep inside, I knew what was going on but I chose to push aside this knowledge. I thought, *not again*, and convinced myself that she was struggling with something that had nothing to do with me. I didn't want to lose another friendship. I had no one else.

One night when we had a bunch of people over, Angie was not acting like herself. I caught her giving me dirty looks and saw her go out of her way to spend time with my husband. Later, I found out that her boyfriend constantly made comments about me to her, to make her jealous, I guess. For some reason, that became my problem and the reason why I was her target. Then, one weekend when I was away visiting family out of town, she took the opportunity to sleep with my husband. That was the end of the friendship—but not the end of my marriage. I kept the man and kicked the female out of my life.

I now see that Angie was also a victim in that crazy mess because she fell for the tactic to separate us. Angie's boyfriend went out of his way to make her feel jealous of me. He was the type of person who had to make his girlfriends feel inferior to other females. The type of man who felt uncomfortable around strong independent women.

One thing I have learned through my lived experience is that when someone is threatened by a friendship, they go out of their way to cause problems in order to separate us. In our case, that was a success.

Conforming

The mindset of toxic femininity has been repeatedly drilled into me since I was very young.

I was brought up in a masculine-dominant house. We had to walk on eggshells so we didn't upset the men in the family.

Women were meant to be 'put together,' with our hair done and nice clothes, and I was taught to *always* put make-up on before leaving the house, even if it was a quick trip to the store down the street. We were expected to stay loyal to the men and always watch our backs when it came to other females. Women were our competition; they were always after what we had. It was common to talk about each other as soon as someone left the room.

It was no different in the workplace. My career was in a masculine-dominant industry where it was not common practice for women to be in leadership roles or even in sales positions. Because of this, the women were cutthroat, always vying for the men's attention, and to be the one who stood out. I was no different. If I wanted to move up in the industry, I had to be that way as well.

Being surrounded constantly by 'Type A' male personalities will do one of two things—you will either retreat or become one of them. Unfortunately, I became one of them. Eventually, I worked my way up to become Vice President in my company, which was almost unheard of for women in my industry. As a result, I had no female friends at the workplace. My motto was, "I'm not here to make friends." Ugh, today that statement makes me cringe.

My company had a couple of locations and I was stationed at our corporate headquarters. I quickly found myself in competition with one of the office workers at the other location, but the crazy thing about this is that I had never met her. We occasionally spoke on the phone for business purposes, but that was it.

The first time I met June was when we held a big corporate meeting at our headquarters. I didn't understand why she kept looking at me then whispering to her coworkers. *Ok, here we go*, I thought, *Obviously, I am going to have some problems with this one*. And boy, did she give me problems.

One of our co-workers from June's location told me she was out for my job *and* was planning on sleeping with my husband. I instantly laughed it off. There was no way she was taking my position from me, and I remember saying if she wanted my husband, that was fine, but she'd best remember who he came home to at night.

My way of thinking was so wrong at that time and I have now raised my standards, but even that aggressive way of thinking and speaking didn't stop June from trying to sabotage my marriage, and me.

My husband also worked with the company and spent a lot of time at her location. She was dating the office manager, and I found out later that he was the motivation for her attacks against me. He encouraged her to try to get me out of the picture, and her in.

Again, here we have June as the true victim, and she didn't even realize it.

Breaking Generational Curses

After my experiences with Mary, Lucy, and Angie, I struggled to connect with other females; it took me years to reconcile that within myself. First, I had to change my mindset and beliefs. I started to pay attention to other females around me who had long-lasting, honest, and real connections with others. To my surprise, I didn't hear any backhanded comments, they didn't talk about one another, and they weren't out for each other's husbands.

This helped me to realize that the problem wasn't with the women at all. We were victims of toxic femininity and were exposed to these social norms at a very young age. It's a mindset that isn't our fault. It's not even our mothers' or grandmothers', or great-grandmothers' fault. It's a toxic way of thinking that has been going on for generations before us and has been passed down throughout the centuries. We have been groomed to think this way.

Talk about an 'A-ha' moment! I realized all my experiences with women, in and out of the workplace, didn't have to be this ball of negative energy filled with toxic traits. Although I didn't realize it at the time, I chose to partake in the downfall of sisterhood. Ouch. That revelation hurt.

But I was no longer going to play that game. Most importantly, I wasn't going to allow my daughters to witness such insane friendships because constant drama and fighting are such a waste of time and space.

I had to learn to be ok with being by myself, and I had to be *my* best friend first. For me (although I'm still working on it), that meant learning to be kind to myself, to give myself some grace, to love myself again, and to forgive *me*. When I was diving deep into healing that part of me, I discovered that I was quite mean to myself and was treating *me* the way others were—the ones I was breaking free from.

Not only did I have to heal from the trauma caused by others, but I also had to do the work to heal from *my own induced trauma*. WOW! What a revelation that was.

I wasn't perfect but this in no way defined who I was or who I am. It's so important that when we find ourselves tangled up in a relationship filled with toxic energy, we retreat as soon as possible! Often, the negative and toxic energy will spread and affect us in ways that we don't expect and, as a result, we tend to make decisions that do not align with who we truly are. It's easy to get sucked into the chaos—then we become the one thing we dread. Toxic.

It's ok to let people go, it's ok to make mistakes, this is how we learn and grow. But it isn't ok to stay in any kind of relationship where there is emotional and mental abuse.

Talking things through in therapy helped to sort out my emotions. After being gaslighted and manipulated for so long by so many people, it took time to get back in touch with my intuition and learn to trust again.

But the true catalyst of change was getting in touch with my spirituality and learning to work with the phases of the moon. Harnessing that energy allowed me to find peace within myself and to trust not only other people but, more importantly, my own intuition.

Learning to discern and to listen to my divine intuition helped me deal with many triggering moments. You may find yourself in situations where fear will start to creep up and you'll think, "they are out to get me." This is where trusting your intuition and using your own discernment is very useful.

I now understand that if someone chooses to cheat or step outside of their relationship, it isn't because of the other person. My ex-husband(s) have cheated on me countless times. If it wasn't with Mary, or Angie, or June, it would have been with someone else. If that is who they are, then they will always find someone else. The problem, I have come to know, is THEM. Plain and simple.

Raising My Vibe

I now share my life with some amazing females and have even reconnected with a couple of women I knew during high school. We enjoy solid, stable, and drama-free relationships. To reach this stage, I had to reset my vibe. Once I started to vibrate on a higher frequency, let go of shame, anger, and hurt, and forgave not only myself but the others who have caused (or tried to cause) me pain, I started to attract the right kind of people in my life.

I have learned what is acceptable to me and what isn't. Now, I have the strength to say, "no," and walk away, and I have gained the wisdom to understand humanity a little better. I act with more compassion and empathy, and have a better understanding of what true sisterhood means. It is more important now than ever before that we start to break the toxic generational chains that bind women and keep us held down.

There is zero regret for meeting the people I have in my life. *Would I do a couple of things differently?* Absolutely. But I am still incredibly thankful for the friendships and relationships I experienced, whether they were for a short span or longer term. They taught me some very valuable lessons, and without them, I wouldn't be the feminine warrior I am today.

I am deeply sorry for any pain I have caused another sister; those actions and behaviors no longer align with my values and I will continue to teach my daughters better and not repeat old patterns.

While I still believe that we do not turn our backs on those we love and care for, we certainly don't have to take their crap either. We can still love them and care for them, but we don't have to get sucked into toxic relationships. It's so important to set boundaries—not only for our happiness and peace of mind but it also helps us retain our own sense of identity.

I get that now.

3

HEALING FROM THE SHADOWS

JENNY ALBERTI

A S I PULLED INTO my driveway, I was filled with fear. I knew something was terribly wrong. My ears began to pound, all I could hear was my heartbeat, and my body was flooded with adrenaline.

I walked up to my front door, put my hand on the handle and, before pushing it open, I closed my eyes. *Please let them still be here*, I pleaded silently.

But they weren't. They were gone.

I grabbed my phone out of my pocket and opened my text messages. "Please bring them back. PLEASE!"

But she wouldn't. I would never see my precious fur babies again.

I wish I'd known when I left the house hours before that it would be the last time I'd see them. I would have told them I loved them one more time. I would have told each of them that they were the best cats any cat-mom could ever hope for.

This was the grand finale of betrayals from my partner of eleven years. She had cleaned out the house and taken my babies with her.

I tell this story for the one who betrayed me just as much as I share it for myself. I tell this story for others who will benefit from hearing it. I tell this story because I see her and hold space for her, and even though I know she'll never read it, my hope is that on some level she'll feel seen and understood.

The concept of betrayal has a significant stigma in society. It's widely agreed upon that it's a terrible thing that one person does to another, and the individual responsible for the betrayal deserves whatever consequences may follow.

The popular sayings, "Karma will take care of them," and, "Revenge is a dish best served cold," suggest that the betrayer should suffer for their actions.

But what if they have been suffering all along? What if they've been tortured on the inside, unable to heal for their entire lives, because they were betrayed as a child?

Let me be clear, I am not saying it's an excuse for someone's awful behavior as they grow older. And I do not justify or condone anyone's terrible mistreatment of another. I firmly believe, however, that perpetuating pain and punishment is not ok.

What truly matters is acknowledging the wounds that are passed from one woman to another, and it is important to promote healing instead. I feel wildly fortunate to have been able to transform the betrayals I endured into an opportunity for personal growth, self-acceptance, abundance, and purpose.

The Pool Party

My niece had just graduated high school and it was time to celebrate. A gorgeous day for a pool party and BBQ, my partner of eleven years and I had celebrated many special occasions with family parties just like this.

For weeks I had been looking forward to a day of fun, sun, and swimming, and as far as I was concerned, all was great for most of the day. There were jello shots and 80s music as family and friends I hadn't seen in years all gathered to celebrate. We played a round of our regular pool game of 'Musical Floaties,' a family favorite.

But then everything went sideways.

I had just started to dig into my delicious BBQ chicken and pasta salad when I decided I was in the mood for a mixed drink to wash it down. My partner and I went inside the house and I suggested we open a bottle of whiskey that had been sitting on the table amidst a collection of other alcohol. We threw some ice in a cup, mixed in some ginger ale then headed back outside.

I offered a taste to my brother-in-law. Little did I know the sip I offered turned out to be from an expensive bottle of whiskey that he had brought with him. A heated exchange of bitter words followed between my brother-in-law and my partner.

My brother-in-law, typically an extremely laid-back and go-with-the-flow kind of guy, was sitting on the patio next to his best friend and my parents, who were enjoying their BBQ ribs. The argument quickly spiraled out of control. My brother-in-law jumped up from his seat, pointing his finger and resorting to name-calling. I was shocked and infuriated; I had never seen him act this way! How dare he? A whirlwind of emotions including confusion, hit me instantly.

Where did this come from? All of this because we opened his whiskey? I remember thinking to myself in the middle of it all.

"You have some fucking nerve!" I shouted back at him in my partner's defense.

My sister quickly came out of the house, attempting to discern what was taking place. I couldn't believe it when she almost immediately took my brother-in-law's side. Surely he was the one out of line, disrespectful, and offensive? The entire situation felt strange, calculated, even premeditated. Why was my sister not even trying to calm me down and talk to me? It was 'us against them' and I didn't understand why.

I couldn't bear to stay at the party a second longer. With a profound sense of urgency, I turned to my partner and said, "It's time to go." In an act of solidarity, my parents rose from their seats simultaneously and affirmed, "Yeah, us too!" With minimal goodbyes, the four of us walked out the front door.

I soon realized I had forgotten the shirt I had worn over my swimsuit, and I had to go back in.

As I opened the front door and stepped inside, I heard my sister talking loudly.

"You've got something to say?" I said to her.

"Yeah, I do!" she snapped back at me.

"Don't care," I said as I grabbed my shirt and blew past her back out the front door. My mind a whirlwind of conflicting emotions, I sat in the passenger seat of my car, utterly beside myself. I cried for the entire hour-and-a-half drive home.

For an agonizing period of two months, a relentless wave of uncertainty washed over me as silence hung between my sister and me, carving a profound fracture in our once-united family. We kept our distance from one another, uncertain if the damage inflicted could ever be healed. With each passing week, an unsettling doubt took over as I questioned everything I had held as unquestionable truth.

A Morning of Clarity

I missed my big sister, so I asked if we could talk. She agreed and we talked for what I initially perceived as two unproductive hours. My sister revealed the anguish she experienced witnessing me in a relationship with someone so cruel and perpetually confrontational. Tears welling up, she expressed her deep concern for my well-being and recounted instances where my partner had subjected me to verbal abuse in front of others, including the painful recollection of my fortieth birthday earlier that year.

Overwhelmed, she implored me to question why I would choose to remain in a relationship with someone who treated me so poorly. In defense of my partner, I cited her tumultuous upbringing, rationalizing that her hurtful words were not truly intended. Little did my sister know the full extent of the mistreatment I endured. No one did.

A few days had passed since our conversation when I found myself seated at the breakfast bar, engaged in writing my morning affirmations—a practice that kept me feeling grounded despite the chaos in my life. Absorbed in my thoughts, I glanced up and saw my partner brewing a cup of coffee.

At that moment, a wave of realization swept over me: she had never shown an interest in how I was coping amidst this chaos. It occurred to me that she may not actually care. Perhaps she was even relieved that things had unfolded this way and was satisfied that I had distanced myself from my sister and brother-in-law.

In the aftermath of the conversation with my sister, a shift occurred within me. Thoughts and emotions churned, prompting an internal dialogue that extended beyond the happenings at the pool party and delved into the depths of my relationship with my partner.

Memories of all the instances where she had been at the heart of disagreements with my family came flooding back, replaying like a vivid movie in my mind.

I was transported back to 2015 when my mother underwent a crucial heart valve replacement surgery. Concern grew among the nurses and my family as she failed to regain consciousness. Instead of offering solace and support during that tense period, my partner initiated disagreements, first with me and then with my father.

Then my mind wandered to our most recent Christmas gathering—raised voices and arguments. My partner's impatience with my family's Christmas Day traditions had forced everyone to expedite unwrapping presents and socialize less because she had work the following morning.

Without fail, this well-worn pattern persisted, infiltrating both family gatherings and the confines of our home. A perpetual cycle of yelling, name-calling, gaslighting, and blame permeated our interactions.

But on that particular morning, as I sat at my breakfast bar, I had a profound revelation: my family had been attempting to protect me. The outburst from my brother-in-law now made perfect sense, as did my sister's support of it.

After eleven long years, the veil began to lift and reveal a truth that had eluded me. It became painfully clear that my partner had been systematically eroding my very essence and I, regrettably, had allowed it to transpire while they stood witness. My family was unable to bear the weight any longer.

The false narrative that my family had betrayed me at the disastrous pool party suddenly collapsed in the presence of truth. The actual betrayal I felt had been inflicted by my partner and by myself, as I had willfully disregarded my own well-being for years. It was at that moment that I acknowledged the urgent necessity for drastic change.

As I reflect upon that conversation with my sister, I realize now that it was not an unproductive exchange; rather, it served as the resounding wake-up call I desperately needed.

"Some people are in such utter darkness that they will burn you just to see a light."

Kamand Kojouri

My partner's upbringing was marked by instability, as her father left the family one Christmas Day when she was a child. She shared with me her profound sense of never truly being loved by all members of her family. Her grandmother had been the nurturing figure she considered as her mother.

As a result of the betrayal, severe trauma, and the subsequent gaslighting she endured at the hands of her own mother, my partner carried wounds that were beyond my comprehension. However, it is not my place to recount her story. What I can share is how far her mother's betrayal cast its shadow, causing a ripple effect that led to my partner betraying me and, in turn, me betraying myself.

The destruction of trust between my partner and her mother caused her to have deep-seated doubts about trusting me right from the start. It was evident that she carried the weight of her past wounds, which drove her to create safeguards to ensure she would never be hurt again.

For the better part of a decade, I endured severe mental, emotional, and physical abuse from her. She relentlessly hurled a barrage of degrading and hurtful names my way, often combining them or adding 'stupid' as a prefix. To cope with the pain caused by her words, I sometimes turned it into a mental game, attempting to guess how many names she could string together in one breath. The phrase "pathetic fat-ass mother-fuckin' piece-of-shit loser" was particularly challenging, yet she managed to utter it effortlessly.

Alongside the name-calling, she repeatedly expressed her wishes for my death, encouraged me to take my own life, and even went so far as to suggest that I should walk onto a freeway. This verbal and psychological abuse became a relentless presence in my everyday life, which systematically eroded my self-worth. It's no wonder that it had such a devastating impact on me.

The attacks seemed never-ending. When the name-calling and suicide taunts lost their effect, she resorted to telling me that no one could ever love me, that I was undesirable and impossible to be with. She insisted that I deserved to be yelled at and even claimed that it was fortunate we didn't have children because I would be a horrible mother.

Then there was the physical aspect: the visible bruises, teeth and nail marks, and the tender lumps on the back of my head from ordinary days turned wrong. In the moments when she recognized the extent of the physical pain she'd caused, she would show her support by offering ice to alleviate the discomfort, or extending a helping hand to assist me in getting back on my feet.

She often told me I was just like her mother, exclaiming, "... and I hate her!" For years this statement left me wondering whether her mistreatment towards me stemmed from a desire to inflict upon me what she wished to do to her mother as a way of seeking retribution for the past.

Through it all, I reassured myself that her treatment of me was a product of her own trauma. I convinced myself that by absorbing everything she directed at me, I was demonstrating my unwavering support and empathy as a partner. I believed that she relied on me because the others in her life had disappointed and abandoned her.

For years, I carried a burden of pain and sadness. I granted her countless pardons, convinced that it was the least I could offer to help her cope with her trauma. While I understood that I couldn't alter her past, I willingly assumed the role of her emotional punching bag, hoping to alleviate even a fraction of her agony. My hope was to provide her with a safe place where she could escape her past.

But it didn't help. It was never enough. No matter what, I could never alleviate her anguish. She remained a wounded young girl, longing for her mother's protection during her most vulnerable moments. She wished her older sister had intervened and stood up for her. More than anything, she simply wanted to have had the experience of being a safe and loved child. As a teenager, she'd moved away from home and navigated the path of survival, all the while suppressing her childhood trauma and burying it as deep as possible. But the weight of her inner darkness only intensified.

She never received the support she needed, and her wounds never had a chance to heal. I understand now that she was in such utter darkness to treat me the way she did; she betrayed and burned me simply grasping at the opportunity to catch a glimpse of light.

The Darkness Behind The Facade

"If I wouldn't go to jail for killing you, I'd have fucking killed you already!"

"You really shouldn't say things like that," I replied, "the cameras record sound, you know."

She responded with no words, only a piercing scream that reverberated off the vaulted ceilings as she charged towards me. She lowered her right shoulder and barreled into me, propelling me through the wall that served as our movie projector screen.

As I freed my injured arm from the new hole in the wall, I told her that my sister, the homeowner, wouldn't hesitate to press charges for property damage if she saw it. In a state of panic, she grabbed the *A Star Is Born* movie poster she had tucked away among other miscellaneous clutter accumulated over the years. Pleading with me to keep it a secret, she pinned up the poster over the hole, assuring me she would have it repaired as soon as possible. Still committed to protecting her, I agreed.

I stared at the poster for a week until she had the wall repaired, fully aware of the truth hidden behind it. I couldn't help but think of how it was a perfect metaphor for our relationship: the façade and the darkness. I couldn't explain this away, sweep it under the rug, move on and pretend that this, too, didn't happen—but I was clueless about how to get out.

In the entire eleven years, my most hopeless moment occurred later that night as I barricaded myself on the bathroom floor, wedged tightly in the corner between the door and the wall. With my knees bent and firmly pressed against the door, I hoped it couldn't be opened. I sat there for hours, crying, because I didn't know what else I could do. Exhausted, I simply couldn't endure any more.

Thankfully, the universe intervened. A few days later, my partner went on a week-long trip and the day after her return, she left for good. No more verbal abuse. No more physical bruises. No more manipulation. No more betraying myself. I could finally take down the façade I had pinned up to conceal the darkness that had consumed my life.

The Transcendence

In the days following my partner's departure, I began to reconcile it all. My beloved pets were gone and my home lay in chaos. But amidst the overwhelming shock and sorrow, I felt a sense of freedom.

When I wasn't cleaning up my house or replacing household items that had been taken, I turned to my journal, where I expressed *a lot*! I had over a decade of pain, shame, anger, and fear to get out of my system. For all those years I continuously suppressed the trauma I was experiencing, pushing it down like it wasn't actually happening.

I also had to deal with the new realization that I had willingly betrayed myself. I didn't know what to do with that reality. I was confused, ashamed, and terribly unsettled that I could have such little self-respect. It rattled me and made me question my own value system. *Did I truly believe in my own values? How could I when my actions betrayed them for so very long?* There was so much for me to work through and untangle while the path ahead was still so uncertain.

Journaling helped so much more than I can express because it brought a profound sense of gratification and clarity. At the end of each journaling session, I tore up the dark thoughts and feelings I had poured onto the paper. I felt that I didn't need them anymore and the act of tearing the words to shreds was also incredibly gratifying.

As time passed, my journaling transformed from a lifeline into a dedicated practice and I transitioned to ending my sessions by setting intentions of what I wanted in my life.

The first thing that I called into my life was a seven-month-old orange tabby cat, whom I named Mango. From the moment I brought him home from the pet store, I was certain everything in my life would be all right. He embodied personality traits from each of the three cats I had lost and, yet, he was also wildly unique. With him around, I began to feel just a little lighter.

One month later, the Women Writing Intentionally Collective LLC was officially formed, marking a significant turning point in my life. This new path I embarked upon has been filled with so much more love, support, and prosperity than I could have ever imagined possible.

As I experience this beautiful transformation, it extends to my relationships, both personally and professionally. Connecting with others authentically was once a struggle, but now I find it easy and effortless, even with strangers.

In particular, my relationship with my sister and brother-in-law has flourished, standing in stark contrast to the day of the pool party. My sister has been by my side and our bond has never been stronger.

Additionally, I have gained clarity in my life's purpose and the meaningful work I want to pursue in this lifetime. Previously, I'd felt completely lost but now I am guided by a clear sense of direction. Every aspect of my life has undergone a deep transformation and I am sincerely grateful for it all.

As I reflect on how far I've come, I find myself filled with profound gratitude for the opportunities that have come my way. It's a remarkable shift from the moments of hopelessness I once experienced curled up on my bathroom floor.

I am a work in progress, and I won't pretend that I'm immune to being triggered. There are days when I must consciously remind myself that the hurtful words spoken to me are not true because, at times, I find myself still believing them.

I understand that healing is not a linear journey where one day all pain will vanish from memory and I, therefore, embrace the fact that I need to provide myself with reminders along the way. Some days are more challenging than others. However, I can confidently say that I have transformed my broken heart into opportunities for growth.

As I navigate the ongoing healing process, I have discovered that the most empowering thing I can do is let go. By releasing resentment, blame, and anger, I have created space for abundance to flow into my life, and I now possess a renewed sense of purpose. I continue to let go through my shadow work practice, allowing for further growth and transformation.

Discovering Shadow Work

When I first started journaling my dark thoughts and feelings, I had no clue what I was doing, nor did I realize there was a name for it. All I knew was that I needed some sort of release, so I turned to the thing I do best—I wrote. Desperate for relief, I found comfort in the act of putting pen to paper, each stroke granting me a momentary respite.

As I stumbled through the early stages of my healing journey, I began to dive into the world of shadow work and the process of integrating my darker aspects. It was through this exploration that I came to understand that my anger, fear, and insecurities—although not inherently negative—were all parts of me, shaped by the trauma I had endured during my eleven-year relationship.

I realized that acknowledging and accepting these aspects of myself were vital steps in my healing process. By accepting these aspects of myself, I wasn't perpetuating them. Rather, I saw the wounds within me, recognized the impact they had on my life—possibly for the first time in my life—and nurtured a space for healing.

Over time, my practice of shadow work has evolved into a more intentional and deliberate practice. Journaling continues to be my preferred method and has become a sacred space. I find a certain power in purging my thoughts with pen and paper, as if the act itself holds a transformative magic.

Insights For Effective Shadow Work Journaling

For those readers who may need it, I want to share with you some insights I learned about journaling in the hope that they may help you on your healing journey. While it's important to emphasize that these tips are not a substitute for professional assistance, they have personally proven valuable in enhancing my own journaling practice and aiding in my self-discovery.

Have No Expectations

Embrace the process of allowing whatever needs to emerge to do so. Try not to filter anything, but instead give yourself permission to write the raw and unfiltered feelings, thoughts, fears, beliefs, and images that need to surface.

Be Curious

In order to let go effectively, you need to be open to exploring and examining so you can uncover the root cause of your fears, beliefs, and judgments. Approach your shadow work journaling with an open heart and a curious mind, ready to unravel what lies unconsciously within.

Observe Without Judgment

As you engage in your shadow work journalling, don't judge the words you write or the feelings you express. That judgment only reinforces the power of the shadow and makes it bigger. Exploring without judgment will provide you with a safe space and a deeper understanding of the hidden parts of you.

Do It Daily

Consistently engaging in a daily practice will help you make steady progress and become more self-aware with each journaling session. Another significant benefit I found in doing it daily was the self-trust it established by honoring my commitment to myself.

Call In Something Different

Releasing is a necessary part of healing. Equally important is the intentional act of calling in what you want instead. Create clear intentions for yourself and for the universe, and indicate you are open to receiving something different than what you are releasing.

Additionally, I recommend finding a quiet space where you can be uninterrupted during your shadow work journalling sessions. Eliminate all distractions and refrain from any technology, other than maybe some meditation music or healing frequencies. I also highly encourage you to light a candle and be in a comfortable position as you write.

I hope these insights help you create a journaling practice that is a source of solace.

Solace and Healing

Everyone deserves to see the light. Everyone deserves to be set free of their torments. Each individual, regardless of their circumstances, should have the opportunity to break free from the relentless grip of what haunts them.

I deserved to be free from my partner's abusive ways. And despite the pain she inflicted upon me, despite the heart-wrenching act of stealing my beloved cats, I acknowledge her own profound need for healing and solace.

While I continue to rebuild my life, I also hold space for the possibility of her own transformation, because she too deserves it. I have no desire for her to endure any more torment—she has already endured a lifetime of it. True solace comes not from revenge, but from the ability to transform our pain and choose a path of empathy, forgiveness, and understanding.

Through my ongoing journey of transforming my personal pain and experiences of betrayal into positive outcomes, I'm not only contributing to my own healing but also actively participating in healing the collective.

By cultivating supportive relationships with other women and holding space for them, I am committed to breaking free of the pattern of hurt, harm, and betrayal, and creating a ripple effect of healing that extends beyond each and every one of us.

We have the power to put an end to the cycle and perpetuation of pain and punishment. It starts with the need for women to work together, trust each other, and commit to healing our own shadows as we embrace the light and shine it as a beacon of hope for those who have not yet found their way out of the darkness.

4

DON'T LEAVE ME FALLING

TERESA FOX

T HE DARKNESS ENVELOPS ME in a warm caress as I lie on the bed. *I can breathe. I am safe.* As the air exhales from my lungs, the warm sting of tears run down my cheeks in an expression of resignation and relief. "I am"—such a small yet powerful statement. I slip into my inner stillness.

Yes, it is still here; a voice inside me stirs—I am here. I haven't abandoned myself. In that one moment when I said, "no more," I found my voice and empowered my fragmented soul to start to heal. In that moment, I gave myself permission and my transformation began.

Seven years earlier, wide-eyed and adventurous, I set off with a vision of a future filled with magic and enchantment. I dreamt of what I would create as I journeyed along roads void of cars, with only the smell of livestock and passing road trains to accompany me. Wind in my hair, a friend by my side; we were both so full of joy and hope for the road that lay before us. The wonder of spirit alive as Lisa and I headed to Outback Australia with the sun on our faces, and the wind whistling through the open car windows, singing and laughing at the adventure that lay ahead

Our adventure started in Melbourne. Both Lisa and I laughed as we ate pizza and packed our little hatchback to begin our trek north. Our destination was all part of the adventure. Neither one of us planners, we were excited by the unknown road waiting to be travelled, the small country towns to immerse ourselves in, and the call of a strong, rich Australian heritage that we longed to explore as we followed the red dirt tracks to anywhere. Neither of us knew this was soon to be but a memory of a time that once was, a friendship soon to be fractured by the heady scent of falling in love.

He was charming, handsome, and said all the right things. His children were a joy; blind to the events that would soon unfold, my heart overflowed with endless love. My intuition squashed as my head justified the red flags that quickly grew. The pain and trauma to follow would not be held by me alone. His reach was vast and his tongue smooth as he seduced all with his promises and words. Isolation and fear were soon to be mine.

I had always wished for a large family but had only been blessed with one child. My prayers had been answered, or so I thought. Unexpectedly, I was blessed with three more beautiful children to raise and love unconditionally.

These children only knew a life so far removed from the way I was raised. It broke my heart to see their living conditions and I was determined to share a new chapter with them, a place filled with magical memories where they could feel safe and learn to be the amazing people I saw inside the hollow eyes that stared back at me.

I had so much love to give—creating a new future for these children, a home filled with love, compassion, and kindness made my heart overflow with joy. I believed this was my forever story. How wrong could I be?

Two years later, I sat in a caravan in far northwest Tasmania and wondered, *How did it get to this point?* The patterns of deceit concealed by ongoing relocations across the country. The pain I felt as I sat alone in the cold dark caravan; pain not only from emotional wounds but also fresh surgical wounds, for which he had no regard. Having never felt so alone, I lay in the cold wishing to die.

A short time earlier the children had been sent to their grandmother's in north Queensland. My heart was broken. I had been betrayed by the family I had come to love.

I tried to explain: I feared surgery so I ran to a shelter because I did not know how to be around his abuse, raise these beautiful children, and recover from major surgery. I thought I was safe, and I was, until four days post-operative when he discharged me from the hospital. *How could I have been so ignorant to not change my next of kin on my forms?* So, without any pain medication, I was dragged to the other side of Tasmania and into complete isolation.

His harsh cruelty cut deeper as the days grew colder. I had to escape. I was dying mentally, spiritually, and if this continued, physically. My trembling hands reached for the phone to call my family. *Would they help? Could they support my escape?*

"Yes, of course," a voice whispered inside. My family had always supported me even if they did not approve of my choices. Finally, I thought I had found the courage to leave. Little did I know this was not the end of our story.

My family welcomed me with open arms as I stepped off the overnight ferry. I spoke with the children regularly and soon forgot his betrayal as I pushed it into an internal locked box, then abandoned myself as I threw away the key and fell, once again, for his charm and lies.

Four months later I moved north to be reunited with the children. My heart was full as I breathed in the warm North Queensland air and prepared for a beach wedding where I would commit to being a family. Life was good. The harsh realities of Tasmania were soon forgotten as we planned our future. The deception appeared to have ceased, but only for a time. He was planning and lying, and creating webs that would eventually come crashing down but, then, life was good.

With our new home situated by the ocean, after work I spent my days on the beach with the children, laughing and playing in our enchanted paradise. The allurement of the ocean captured my imagination daily and I felt alive and free for the first time in years. My guard was down; I was unaware that this was merely the calm before the storm.

A cyclone was coming—and with it came the truth. The intensity of the storm was foreboding as we bunkered down in our home in fear as we had never experienced a cyclone before. He was absent, and the truth of his whereabouts enlightened us to what was really going on. He was not at work but living a life of deceit and lies. Once more, my heart was broken and I was betrayed by the man I trusted and loved. This was the final straw. *No more!* I escaped.

The darkness that influenced me at this time in my life gave me the courage to step into my wisdom. I began to find integration in my life and learn to live in a state of ease and grace. I had felt so separated from myself, my wisdom, and my power. The only thing I had left was my multi-sensory perception, which told me this experience was merely part of my soul's evolution.

My soul chose this journey to heal past traumas. Shame and guilt had been my companions for so long, and I had blamed myself for all the events in my life that had caused me pain. I was living as a victim and, until I changed my internal dialogue, there I would stay.

My upbringing was a very different experience from the one I had recently escaped. Every day, I am grateful for my courage and tenacity; they kept me going in my darkest hours. This repeated betrayal gave me the gift and drive to create a life beyond my wildest dreams.

My path was initially one of my own stubbornness and wilfulness as I stopped listening to my inner guidance and tried to steer my soul in another direction. When I let go, my whole world changed and I found my path, my tribe, and most importantly, myself.

I connected to my soul as it ebbed and flowed like waves against the shore with no beginning and no end. I stepped into a place of healing. My journey gained momentum as I moved into the next chapter of my life with purpose, action, and intention. Finally, I could breathe again and thus began my breathwork, meditation, and healing odyssey.

Through healing others as a multi-modality energy healer, mindset coach, mental health and addictive behaviour clinician, I also heal myself. I use my understanding of the human mind and my passion for living life to the fullest to empower myself in creating mind, body, and soul connection to uncover the most authentic version of self.

I have learned to create change in my life and continue to ask myself, "What else is possible?" These opportunities have benefited me as I've stepped into consciousness. I love that I get to live in a state of compassion, grace, and love—and I live by these three beliefs because three has always been 'my number.' I find such freedom in these statements:

Life is too short to do something that doesn't bring you joy.

We are all perfectly imperfect beings and should not be afraid to show our flaws.

I am in control of my thoughts, actions, and destiny.

My healing journey continues on a daily basis. Each day I am filled with gratitude for the magnificent life I have created. I am grateful to be here to tell my story as there were many times my family and friends were in fear for my life. I survived. I am not a victim; I am a warrior.

I now support other women to step into their authentic power and wisdom, to have a voice, be heard, and not live in fear. I support women to activate authentic change, to transform, self-discover, heal and renew, reset and activate, and align and anchor. Through my work I, too, get the opportunity to heal on a daily basis. For any woman who relates—I hear you, I see you. You have a voice and you deserve to be heard.

5

FAITHFUL TO ME

WELLA LILES

HAVE YOU EVER BEEN the girl who follows all the rules? The girl who doesn't mind discomfort for the sake of peace? The girl who bites her tongue because, in her mind, that's the right thing to do? The girl who can't wait to please everybody because that's how she thrives?

In short, the girl who lives on everybody else's expectations, but hers. Amidst all that, have you ever made a choice that shatters your beliefs, only to realize it will ultimately lead to your greatest discovery—yourself?

To say it is difficult is an understatement. I was there a few years ago. I was that girl. Honestly, I couldn't have imagined how my life could be different. Sometimes, I can't help thinking that I'm still that girl, but the exception is that I now make it a point to be mindful of my decisions.

You see, I once had this so-called picture-perfect family life. A beautiful son. A loving husband whom I met while serving in the military. A thriving nursing career with all the bells and whistles, and a nice three-bedroom house complete with two family dogs to top it off.

My life was bliss without the white picket fence, and the people around me never failed to remind me of that fact: "You're so lucky, Wella. Not everyone gets to marry their first boyfriend and go on to have this perfect life."

Deep down, things were far from perfect. I didn't know what it was or what could have caused it, but I felt disconnected from my husband and the only relationship I'd ever known. Don't get me wrong, our marriage was not toxic in any way. He was simply there.

It was a strange feeling to realize that I didn't know him and he didn't know me, at least not in the way that I wished. I felt like our relationship stayed on the surface despite my years of attempting to get to know each other on a deeper level.

This feeling didn't happen overnight. Rather, it was gradual, carefully taking years to unfold until I woke up one morning wondering where the time had gone. I asked myself, after all these years, despite this strange, overwhelming feeling: *Do I make a decision that is right for me, even though it is not in the eyes of my parents, friends, siblings, cousins, neighbors, and relatives?*

Suddenly I felt bad to even question what might have been the best thing that ever happened to me. *Is this a normal phase of married life that I just can't handle? Is it because I'm tired of my work-life situation? Should we go to counseling to explore these things? Should I simply choose to do my very best to be happy because it is what I'm supposed to do? Is it the pressure of keeping up with this picture-perfect life?*

I held all these questions within me to protect the truth I had been scared to admit for a very long time. Our relationship was complete, but I didn't want to let go. I didn't want to hurt him, or anybody. I did not want to lose the 'good girl' image that had defined me. Most of all, I feared what other people would think if they learned how I truly felt. The inner conflict nagged me for the longest time, and it didn't feel good.

And so began my ordeal of finding emotional connection outside my marriage, which eventually led to a couple of affairs. All because I wanted to know what it was like to be with someone else, to feel connected and 'brand new' again. I lived a secret double life, while hiding behind this perfect façade of a happy, loving wife and mother, so I could stop merely existing, fill the empty spaces in my life, and start to feel like myself again.

In my mind, I was 'getting my fix' and coming back to the 'complete' person I had not been in a while, then going home to my family feeling like myself again. That was all that mattered. I thought to myself, *It's not like I'm disregarding my priorities.*

In fact, I handled my business exactly as I should, and always had. My husband and child were taken care of. The bills were paid. I somehow managed to have a career and still be the ideal homemaker: cooking, doing laundry, cleaning, grocery-shopping, and running all the errands to ensure the house was well kept. I even had a side-hustle selling oils.

My extra-curricular activities were only temporary, and the world need not find out about them, as I figured they would be over before I knew it.

Except they were far from over. No, not even close. To my surprise, my unfaithfulness led me to fall intensely in love with someone else. Sometimes, no matter how hard we try to hide them, secrets are meant to be discovered. My then-husband was broken and angry while my marriage and everything I worked hard for hung by a thread.

But, despite being overwhelmed with conflicting emotions of shame, guilt, sadness, and fear, I was determined to fix the brokenness I caused.

At the same time, I felt highly conflicted and more disconnected than ever.

Why was I trying so hard to fight for a marriage that I knew was not working and would never work? When I chose to believe that we could move forward, I also knew I would always be reminded of the things I'd done.

"But Wella, this was all your fault," a concerned friend of mine once said, "If you want your marriage to work, you need to do what it takes, bend over backwards, accept the imminent harsh treatment, do whatever he tells you to do and be ok with that. That's how you gain his trust back."

In my mind, this was not ok. Taking their advice was the fastest way to completely lose myself all over again—and never get me back. Yes, I was sad. The guilt ate me alive. Working on my marriage because we made a vow to each other was the right thing to do and what was expected of me.

I was faced with a difficult decision that would change my life forever, and I knew I had to make my choice. If I stayed, I would always feel unhappy, but everyone around me would be pleased. If I left, I would burn bridges, break my husband's and son's hearts and maybe, possibly, pursue a new relationship that felt right for me on all levels. However, that relationship was not a guarantee, and I realized I might end up by myself if things didn't work out. Regardless, I knew my life would never be the same.

Every decision comes with risks, no matter what you do. You must simply decide if it's a choice worth making. I chose to let go and embrace the unknown. *Was I afraid?* Damn right I was. *Was it messy?* Of course; changes are never meant to be smooth sailing to begin with. *Did I burn bridges along the way?* Most definitely. But I realized that people who choose to stay in your life, whether they agree with your decisions or not, are meant to be there. The rest does not matter.

Yes, I cheated on my ex-husband. I was that woman. But I'm not only that woman.

I do not celebrate cheating nor condone it to solve problems. But I acknowledge that people can fall into this trap. I understand that sometimes people make mistakes and stray from their commitments, for whatever reason. It takes a lot for a woman to take this drastic step. Especially for women, who face double standards in society and have to deal with twice the shame and ridicule a man faces when he cheats.

Cheating is not just a result of boredom and unhappiness, but rather a combination of feeling disconnected, undervalued, unappreciated, and in all kinds of emotional turmoil, all of which I have felt many times in my previous marriage. It takes a lot of courage for a woman to stand by her decisions and face the consequences, even if it means losing the support you thought you once had.

Self-forgiveness is never easy, but it was necessary. The truth is that I failed to recognize the one person I betrayed most in this affair—myself. Some relationships run their course and it is ok to move on. Instead of dwelling on the 'what-ifs,' I made a conscious choice to focus on the path that was clearly right in front of me; a path filled with a newfound love and the three little ones who have sprung from that love.

Life is a gift that you must cherish every day. Have faith in yourself and don't let the pursuit of perfection consume you. You are not defined by your choices or mistakes, but understand that sometimes this journey of life requires you to make decisions that will hurt yourself or others. This is how you grow and truly discover yourself.

I spent most of my life trying to please everyone, and honestly, sometimes I still do. But when I started to live truthfully, I found genuine peace. Remember this as you go through your own transgressions and transformations, no matter how messy it gets.

Take a deep breath. Trust yourself. Keep going. It will be ok. You will be ok.

6

DISCARDED BOTTLES AND PAPER PLATES

RUTH FAE

I WAS ABUSED AS a child. Sexually. Emotionally. Secretly. Little-me did an amazing job of protecting me, saving me from the ongoing and inevitable heartbreak, but she was irrevocably wounded. Betrayed.

This betrayal is felt on so many levels. As a fifty-year-old woman, I have peeled back the layers for over half of my life. Sometimes quickly tearing the scab off the wound and facing the pain, the blood, the rawness. Other times I've been more careful, peeking beneath the Band-Aid of my self-protection and gently probing the wound, searching for a way to bring those separated pieces of my soul back together.

The effect of this betrayal manifested itself in so many ways. Self-doubt. Lack of self-worth. Imposter Syndrome. Looking in the mirror and wondering who the hell is looking back at me. Sometimes I feel an incredible disconnect from my younger self. Sometimes I feel like I have betrayed myself way more than anyone else did. I repressed the memories so I didn't have to live the experience of betrayal over and over again—and while I can now thank Little-me for protecting me in the only way she could, it can often be hard to see through the fog to discover who I truly am.

Music helps. The other day my partner played an album from my childhood that I haven't listened to in forty years, yet I still know every word, every beat drop, every backup 'ooh' and 'ahh.' Even as I laugh outwardly, inside I wonder how that's even possible when I don't remember so much more.

Music takes me back to the happy times. Driving to visit my cousins, belting out Bucks Fizz, Abba, and John-fucking-Denver. Impromptu bedroom concerts with Elizabeth, a close friend who, at eleven, was three years older than me and a font of grown-up information about concepts I shouldn't have knowledge about yet, tragically, did. Concepts that, paradoxically, I needed and wanted to understand, yet didn't.

Looking back, I can hear the soundtracks of my childhood. Albums that represent life stages where memories can't. The freedom of pedalling madly to see my friends in the Melbourne bayside suburb of Black Rock—my teenage haven—while the *Dirty Dancing* soundtrack blasted through my Walkman. I've always been drawn to songs of passion, of love, of connection—but not of betrayal.

In a wordless-yet-noisy rebellion, understood by generations of teenagers across the globe, I hid in my room playing *1996 Just for Kicks* and Transvision Vamp's *Pop Art* on endless repeat purely to annoy my parents. *Barry Bissel's American Top 40* was the Sunday night highlight of my week as I lay on my bed for hours, ready to press 'record-stop-record-stop' to create the ultimate mix-tape of the thoughts, feelings, and questions I did not have the answers for.

The music of my childhood, teens, and twenties rarely transports
me to sadness. Sure, the odd break-up song reminds me of endless
tears wetting my pillow as I silently sobbed in my room. It was
the soundtrack to writing the jumbled-up, scrappy poetry of angsty
self-expression that I tucked away in my wardrobe.

But these memories now come with compassion for that broken,
hurt teenager. They are softened by the years and bigger heartbreaks.
Now, I am pleased to have those memories—especially when so
much else is missing.

That's the thing about recovering repressed memories. *Do we trust
them? How do we trust them?*

As a survivor, this is something I've explored time and time again. It's
driven me insane. When the first memory first came back—a "What
the actual fuck?" moment if ever there was one—I was desperate for
answers.

At twenty-three, I had so many questions during my weekly visits
to the Centre Against Sexual Assault. Visits where my counsellor
became my lifeline and saviour in some of the darkest moments of
my life. *Are these memories real? Am I making them up? Why the fuck
would I make them up?*

For a while, these questions were much bigger than the 'whats' and
'whys' of the actual abuse. *How do I trust myself? My brain? My
recollections?* I was so fucking scared to tell anyone about them in case
they didn't believe me. *How could I expect them to believe me when
what I remembered was beyond belief?*

As I searched for answers to questions I couldn't even verbalise, I re-
searched, read, and devoured stories of other people's experiences. Solace

and a level of acceptance came in the form of a book, *Breaking the Silence,* by Liz Mullinar and Candida Hunt.

In the chapter, *Recovering Memories*, the authors explain that, *"the process called 'forgetting' takes place to protect our vulnerable and over-whelmed child from the full horror of an agonising experience. They come as experiences detached from meaning, flashes of images without cause, nightmares without apparent foundation, tastes, sounds and bodily sensations without stimulus, fears and uncontrollable feelings. And all the old demons of our childhood return: self-hatred, despair, self-accusation. No accuser could equal the ferocity with which most survivors at first reject their own memories."*

This explanation, and the subsequent survivors' stories, helped me to recognise what had happened in my brain, and why. But it didn't help me to manage the hurt, anger, or the thought that I had betrayed myself. Every returning memory challenged my perception of who I was and, for a long time, I experienced a strong feeling of disconnection from my true Self.

So, in a desperate struggle to manage this ferocity of emotion, I wrote. So much. Pages and pages of confusion, sadness, and trauma poured out in expressions of pain and anger, not only for my abuser(s), but myself.

While this initial period of intense questioning passed within a couple of years, my deep-seated lack of self-love and feelings of not being worthy or good enough have continued to haunt me.

During the past twenty-five years, I've searched for help (and acceptance) from friends, medical professionals, alternative healers, and spiritual guides. I've talked to my sister, and a select few other family members. I've "disclosed" so many times. But maybe not as many as I'd wished.

Numerous times, I've silently screamed with the burning desire to 'tell.' Not only to share my story and reach for help and understanding, but also to move through the personal barrier of secret keeping, the 'don't tell or you'll get in trouble' belief that is synonymous with silencing the voices of the abused.

Sometimes the words simply don't come—from fear of not being heard, of not being believed, of being discounted or belittled. And when they do come, people often don't know how to respond. *How can they when even I don't know how to respond to such a horrible truth that lies within me?* Some people simply can't believe. Some won't. Some ask for details—often details I can't give.

The betrayal of a child's trust in adults and the subsequent distorted ability to trust their own bodies and minds is huge. Life-changing. Personality-altering. But where does it fit in with the 'sister wound'? And how did I transform such pain into 'opportunities for healing, growth, and abundance'?

Ultimately, this is a story about patterns. Thought patterns, behavioural patterns. Societal patterns and conditioning. And how understanding those internal and external patterns can lead us to grow and learn who we are at our core. Then, in turn, how this awareness can lead to transformation, healing, and abundance.

Thirteen Reasons – *What?*

I was raped at sixteen. But I didn't even recognise it as rape until I was forty-three, while watching *Thirteen Reasons Why* with my teenage son. The final episode of Season One was when it hit me.

I sat on the couch in shock, frantically trying to hide the fat tears rolling down my cheeks. I desperately didn't want my son to make the link. To understand why I was crying. And when he went off to bed, I didn't know how to speak my truth.

Although I have spoken about this situation since then, it wasn't until only a few days ago while discussing similar experiences with a dear friend (and worrying about our teenage daughters) that I remembered—and truly understood—the painful, messy details of before, during, and after.

It was the 'after' that damaged me the most.

Passed out on the couch, a nineteen-year-old boy (man?) I had a massive crush on, sexually assaulted me. Other people were in the room while it happened; I still wonder what on earth they were thinking.

I only have flashes of the actual rape, but I have very clear memories of trying to fight him off, of screaming "NO" in my head. I have no idea if I spoke the actual words, but I know I didn't want to have sex. And the rest is blank—until I woke up the next morning under a blanket on the couch with my jeans undone, bra askew, and a horrible pain in my groin.

Luckily, the offender was asleep in his room, so I gathered myself together just enough to leave and go to a friend's house to investigate 'the damage.'

Two girls came with me. Both sixteen. Both in what is now viewed as unhealthy relationships with 'older boys.' When I told them what happened, I didn't say that I was raped. Confused, sore, and hungover, I didn't even *see* it as rape. I said, "I had sex with…" And here is where the unintentional, yet damaging, betrayal of sisterhood occurred.

They were frustrated with *me*. He had just started seeing another girl. *What? I didn't know that!* If she found out, then it would upset the balance of our friendship group.

They were angry with *me*: "What if you're pregnant? What if you get an STD?" He was a player after all, and I had no idea if he'd used a condom.

The word 'rape' didn't come into it. To all of us, I was completely in the wrong.

Back in the 1990s, there was much less open awareness about 'consent' than there is nowadays. It was my fault because I was drunk, I was 'available,' and everyone knew I thought this boy (man?) was gorgeous.

And let me make this clear, I thought *exactly* the same as my friends. In common parlance, I 'slut-shamed' myself. I blamed myself. I was angry with myself. And I was fucking terrified.

So, in the interest of 'keeping the peace,' 'doing the right thing,' and 'holding my head up high,' my friends and I went back to the house where the party had been held to help clean up. By doing this, we were showing that everything was cool, that I was cool. Such a cool customer.

Hah! I cleaned the very room I had been assaulted in. Picked up discarded bottles and paper plates. And with every piece of rubbish, my heart broke a little more and my sense of isolation increased.

As party-goers began to wake up, I felt the side-eyes and heard the whispers. Of course, I acted the part; no, there was nothing wrong. I'm cool, remember? *Did I have sex with him? Yeah sure, what of it?* False bravado masked every knife wound—and the burning pain in my pants.

Eventually, he came out of his room with the girl he was dating. Everyone looked at me, and at him. There was a tangible pause, an uncomfortable silence; I took one look at this 'beautiful, mature' couple who depicted everything 'young, stupid, ugly me' felt I was not—and fled.

At home that afternoon I lay on my bed and cried. Listening to Kate Ceberano's *Bedroom Eyes* over and over again, I unconsciously convinced my psyche that Michael and I had 'broken up,' that he had left me for this other girl who was everything I was not.

I turned my fear and pain into something I understood. Something that was socially acceptable. I could understand feeling 'like a fool' as a dumped, ugly sixteen-year-old. I could not put 'I was raped' into a concept, let alone words. My psyche, through the conditioning of abuse, had trained me to reframe, reword, and make it my fault. To betray myself.

Should I have arrived at a party after a twelve-hour shift and tried to 'catch up' with the people who had been drinking since 7pm? No, probably not, but that was 'what we did.' It was expected of me; we all expected it of each other. Midori Illusions, our drink of choice, were thrust into my hands. I hadn't eaten. I weighed next to nothing and was a 'cheap date'—the clichéd 'two drinks and she's anyone's!'

Can you see how the common thoughts and words used supported these internalised beliefs? In 2023, my teens would call their friends out if they spoke like that. But we were conditioned, we blindly repeated words we grew up hearing, and most of us had never been taught to challenge our own conventions.

Get upset about apartheid? Absolutely. Stand up against the 'gay killings' of the 1980s? Yes! But question our own culture, society, and social bubble? Nope! It simply wasn't done.

School on Monday sucked. On the way there, I stopped at a phone box and made an appointment to see the doctor to get the morning-after pill. All day, while fending off comments that only increased my feelings of isolation and pain like, "What? Ruth had sex with a nineteen-year-old? But she's such a nerd," I prayed that it wasn't too late.

That afternoon, I had to tell my family doctor that I'd had unprotected sex. In the immediate post-AIDS period, this was unforgivable, and so I received a long lecture about 'safe sex'—while in my head I felt a huge discordance. In hindsight, maybe safe sex should have been amended to 'safe rape'? Should I have carried a condom at sixteen to make sure my rapist didn't give me an STD—or a baby? That's, of course, if I was actually conscious.

I'm not mad at my friends. While I see that we were all working within the patterns our upbringing and society drummed into us, the sense of being betrayed by my friends, my sisters—for want of a better word—still haunts me. The way that they, and the rapist, just tossed me aside like some used and grotty paper plate is, almost, a forever wound.

And yet, I can still see that we were conditioned to keep the peace. Don't rock the boat. Girls are temptresses, sinners. It's our fault. We 'ask for it.' *But do we?*

Asking For It

Things are different now and kids are taught about body safety, and consent by parents, teachers, and each other. Yet in Australia, sexual assault of and by teens is still on the rise.

According to the Australian Bureau of Statistics, *"There were a record 31,000 sexual assaults reported in Australia in 2021, a rise of 13% in one year. Experts say more women are reporting crimes, but opportunities to commit assaults are also increasing. The majority of people reporting assaults were under 18, sparking calls for better education and services for young people."*[1]

It blows my mind that my daughters still face the same threats I did as a teenager. I want to keep them safe, but I can't. *How can I when I couldn't keep myself safe?*

Thankfully, my girls have brothers, and we all share incredibly open and honest conversations around the dinner table so, hopefully, my daughters are more aware and less trusting than I was. Hopefully my sons will always call out questionable or threatening comments and behaviours when they hear and see them. And hopefully, they will all protect and support each other, their friends, and continue to speak up and fight to raise awareness about any abuse they encounter in their lives and communities.

But even with all these positives, they are still at risk. Drinks get spiked. 'One too many' is an easy mistake to make. And rapists still rape.

#MeToo, and Three, and Everyone

My forty-three-year-old revelation that I had been raped came around the time Tarana Burke's #MeToo movement was on the rise internationally. Women had started to talk. Stories of assault became the norm as many of us opened up for the first time about an inappropriate teacher, peer, or family member.

Every single one of my friends had *at least* one story to tell. It was horrifying. How much damage has been done? But what also became apparent in the face of #MeToo is that so many women, (including me), had no idea how to support each other. Not really. Not deep down.

We were so conditioned to 'suck it up' and 'push through' that while we listened, hugged, and wiped the tears of release, we had no idea how to actively help each other shift the pain.

Echoes

At the start of 2020 I left my marriage, and my home. My world imploded and, suddenly, I was sending my kids to their dad's every second week. Sunday nights were the hardest—when grief hit the strongest. Just as our wider world had become pandemically-unrecognisable, so had mine.

I've always tried to give my children what I did not receive as a child. Safety, stability, consistency. Unquestionable love. Then that was whipped out from under them—or at least, that was how I viewed it. The guilt I felt was extreme.

On top of this guilt, I was sad, grieving, worried, and questioning everything I did, thought, and felt. My inherent insecurities raised their heads—self-doubt and lack of worth again became prominent figures in my psyche as I struggled with this new and strange world.

Like most women, I turned to my female friends, my long-time 'besties,' to help me understand. To work through the questions, explore my thoughts, and help me figure out who the hell I am.

I will be forever grateful to the handful of women who stood by me and listened, advised, and supported me with grace and unfailing honesty. Even when they didn't understand or disagreed with my choices, they asked questions, challenged my beliefs, encouraged me to seek the help I needed, and gave me the space to figure my shit out. These women rock!

But, as with being raped at sixteen, I was also met with fakery, shaming, dismissiveness, and actual abandonment. The parallels are stark and cold. Lifelong friends, who had once trusted me with their children and dark secrets, simply up and left. And that betrayal gutted me.

How could I break up my family? How could I hurt my ex like this? How could I...? They are all valid questions, but they don't take into account that there is mutual responsibility involved in the demise of a relationship. I left, therefore 'all of the things' were my responsibility. Just as when I was drunk and 'available,' being raped had also been my responsibility.

Was the childhood abuse my responsibility too?

I believed this for a long time—in fact, even after years of therapy, deep dives into my psyche, tears, and pain as I tried to 'make sense of it all' and 'let go,' I still struggle with this concept. Experiencing sexual assault as a child made me feel dirty, shameful, and false. I played the game and put on a brave face for years as I people-pleased and tried to fit in, while constantly living in fear that those very 'people' I loved would see the real, ugly, damaged me who lived inside.

It was my fault. I wasn't enough.

Although it's still sometimes a challenge, thankfully I no longer believe this. I now see that the blame, the betrayal, the shame, and the guilt lies in the hands of abusers, and of the people who turn a blind eye. But their ultimate betrayal of my safety, innocence, and trust led to further betrayals as I, and my teenage (and adult) friends, tried to cope with situations that we had not been taught to manage.

As I grew up, became a wife and mother, and took on all the other roles that we bear in our lives, I tried to understand. I've spoken with counsellors, psychologists, and healers in an attempt to make sense of my experiences and myself. But it was not until the last few years that I've truly begun to learn how deep societal conditioning runs and how these once-accepted words, behaviours, and actions have systematically created patterns that allow abuse to be seen as the fault of the abused.

Like so many other people who internalise hurt, shame, and guilt, in my younger years I rebelled, lied, made some very poor choices, and put myself in dangerous situations. Then, as I matured, I lived a good, healthy life. On the surface, things were pretty wonderful, and I've been genuinely happy and fulfilled. But deep inside lurked pain that desperately needed to be acknowledged and healed.

All Better?

This brings up another point, another betrayal of sorts. The first counsellor I ever saw, the one who helped me when my repressed memories came back with a vengeance, told me after a few months of sessions that I was 'healed.' At the time, I thought that was brilliant news—and even went out for dinner to celebrate!

With the wisdom of another twenty-five years of life experience, I now feel that she chose her words poorly. I understand that I was 'doing better,' was no longer thinking the world would be a better place without me in it, and that I had begun to put some healthy boundaries in place with unhealthy people in my life. But I was far from healed.

Five years later, while pregnant with my first child, I was assailed by fearful thoughts that my childhood experiences would prevent me from being a good mother. When my son was born, I became filled with anger that anyone, anywhere, could possibly hurt an innocent child. I knew I would defend and protect my child in every way possible, so it did not make sense to me that other adults could, and did, hurt children.

Then a few years later, the birth of my first daughter brought another round of heightened emotion as I was terrified about bringing a girl into the world. *What if she was ever hurt as I had been?* These thoughts and feelings were incredibly difficult to reconcile, and I had to do a lot of work to process and manage all the emotions that arose.

I realised then that I wasn't completely healed from the trauma of abuse. These significant life changes threw challenges, fears, and threats into my path. And, as a result of the "You are healed" comment, it took me a long time to understand that I wasn't going insane, I wasn't broken, and that people who have experienced abuse often feel this way during pregnancy and when becoming a parent.

It took me significantly longer—and much more therapy—to realise that these feelings never fully disappear and that the hurt never truly goes away. But I've learned that it is possible to process emotion safely and gently, to give voice to my fears and beliefs—however ugly they may feel—and to be seen, heard, and accepted for the imperfectly perfect person I am.

This knowledge has finally led me to a deep inner understanding that, in this life, I am OK. Maybe better than OK. I am whole, I am happy, I am loved—and it's a good feeling.

I often used to wonder who I would have become without the patterns created in childhood that were reinforced throughout my life. This worried me greatly until I began to explore my spirituality, understand more about masculine and feminine energies, and my eyes were opened to the societal conditioning that we, as humans, often adhere to without question.

The generational trauma that is passed on through families, not to mention centuries of power-plays, religious beliefs, and patriarchal rulership, have all played a part in why we, as humans, do what we do. Once this understanding fell into place, I began to view the world, and myself, differently. And that, in turn, changed the way I felt about the betrayals I have experienced throughout my life.

Although I sometimes still struggle to verbalise the concept, I now see the people who betrayed me did so because of the hurt *they* have experienced. This doesn't excuse their choices or their actions—they will have to carry their own feelings about this throughout their lives—but this 'inner knowing' leaves me free to figure out and stand in the truth and beliefs that I create, for me and no one else.

Tuning In

My fears about not being a 'good mum,' or worries about my children being hurt led me to do the work to break these cycles. My children gifted me with the opportunity and awareness to build a life where they felt loved, safe and secure, part of a community, and, most importantly, seen and heard. A life where they are not afraid to have a voice.

I know this is not always easy for them and that as they move through life they will face their own challenges, pain, and betrayals, but they understand the inherent value of open, honest communication and connection with themselves as well as others.

Their childhoods were, and still are, filled with friendship and community. Our home has an open door, so their friends are always welcome to pop in and out, and now that they are older, even come to stay if they need to. They and their friends know that I will *always* be there to listen, support, and help, no matter what's gone wrong in their lives. No matter what mistakes they've made, our home offers solace and a safe space to stop, regroup, and begin to heal.

Music has played a huge role in my family life, too. No longer constrained by the vagaries of radio DJ's and mixed-tapes, we have family playlists for every era of their lives. We sing in the kitchen, in the car, and when we snuggle on the couch. We love going to concerts and shows.

And our family playlists certainly featured strongly during the two years of incessant lockdowns we experienced in Melbourne. That time of incredible worldwide uncertainty that coincided so painfully with their parents' separation was filled with laughter and tales of 'remember when' as we reminisced to the songs of their childhood—a beautiful reminder of the safety and comfort they grew up with.

---◦✦◦---

One Foot in Front of the Other

During the past three years my own transformation, while still an often-messy work in progress, has played out in a series of challenges and fascinating synchronicities.

As much as I may have emotionally kicked, screamed, and resisted, I've had to learn to move with and through the damage of betrayal, and embrace the lessons it has brought.

A serious accident in mid-2022 taught me to accept being helped and cared for. I had to rely on other people, I had no choice—but I, again, have been gifted the opportunity to face my fears head-on, and do it with grace and compassion for myself, rather than blindly forging ahead, 'pushing through,' and 'keeping going' as I have done in the past.

This experience, as much as it sucked, has shown me that the unconscious patterns of my earlier years no longer serve me, and I had to make the conscious choice to be open to change and to accept the love, help, and support that I so readily give others but never felt deserving of.

Completely unable to walk for over six months, I battled feeling 'trapped' and 'unable to escape' which no doubt led to the resurfacing of a few more repressed memories.

Thankfully, I have a fabulous support system in place (and years of practice) so, while it wasn't fun by any means, I knew I was safe and equipped with the tools to face the 'ugly' and allow the emotions to move through me until they couldn't hurt anymore.

I learned to 'lean in,' to allow my body and mind to feel and process the memories as they arose, and this knowledge has given me the courage and freedom to explore who I am at my core.

And it is no coincidence that as my body physically healed, I travelled a deep journey of emotional and spiritual growth and transformation.

The Magic of Storytelling

It is also no coincidence that my work has also rapidly evolved during the past few years. While working as a copywriter, I was incredibly conscious of learning, understanding, and staying true to the 'voice' of my clients in their written and spoken content.

But, as I stepped into my true purpose, coaching writers and authors to write their books, tell their stories safely and confidently, and move through their fears of judgement, I clearly see the healing—individual and collective—that comes when silenced voices share their life experiences.

Storytelling *is* music. It has rhythm. It flows and has a vibration and frequency that resonates with the people who need to hear it the most. Sharing our stories of betrayal, pain, and how we can transform our experiences to bring healing and abundance into our lives lets other people know they are not alone. More than anything, for those of us in the depths of despair, who do not trust anyone—least of all themselves—hearing the words of another brings a sliver of light, and hope.

When it comes to listening to other people, especially when they talk about rape and assault, we—as a collective—can do better. We can make conscious choices that are free from judgement and choose how to respond in a way that supports the abused rather than the abuser.

We can choose to question the status quo, conditioning, and patterns that plague our society, and be led by our own sense of fairness, compassion, and humanity. We can and *should* (I don't use this word lightly) call out people who do harm. In doing this, we all have the ability to change the patterns held within and without.

If we listen and *hear* the words being spoken, as well as be aware of the energy that accompanies them, only then we are free to respond from our hearts rather than our heads. And, as in the case of the beautiful people who have supported me through my journey of transformation, we can also be open to recognise and call out our loved ones when they harm themselves. Because through our conditioning and corresponding beliefs, thoughts, habits, and actions, sometimes we do, however unintentionally, betray our true selves.

As a child, teenager, and adult, I was betrayed. Badly. I am also keenly aware that during my life I have betrayed other people, as well as myself. But I have also come to realise that I have protected and saved myself many times over. My brain and body simply did what they needed to do to look after me, and I no longer fight the memories. In unravelling the patterns created by abuse and conditioning, I have learned so much about myself and our world, my internal and the external universe.

Although I still sometimes feel like that uncertain sixteen-year-old girl, as I consciously bring the pieces of my soul back together, I step into my wisdom and embrace my powerful purpose in life. I no longer feel discarded, like some day-old party trash. I'm learning to speak, to shout, to sing. And the music is sweet.

--◦❖◦--

If you live in Australia and need support regarding sexual assault please contact:

Family and domestic violence support services:

- 1800 Respect National Helpline: 1800 737 732

- Women's Crisis Line: 1800 811 811

- Men's Referral Service: 1300 766 491

- Mensline: 1300 789 978

- Lifeline (24-hour Crisis Line): 131 114

---

1. Khadem, Nassim "Sexual assault reports in Australia hit all-time high. What's driving the increase?" ABC News Posted online: Friday 29 July 2022

7

THE DISCOVERY OF SELF-BETRAYAL

Amanda Norr

WHEN I HEAR THE words *betrayed* or *betrayal*, I think of pain, intention, and the damage that follows. I have found that, even when it is innocent and unintentional, it is still just as damaging.

Based on my life experience, I found myself questioning what I could actually add to the conversation. Married at eighteen, I didn't attend formal schooling past high school, nor have I sought to build any kind of career. I feel very sheltered in many ways.

The sister wound of betrayal, however, runs deep in our subconscious. My perspective over the last few years is that our society functions and has built a foundation based on this wound. The systems of power can't maintain their structure unless upon the backs of women.

So many amazing women have taught and shaped me as I have grown. Looking from the outside in, I have had such a good life, yet I have stumbled and suffered. I have had to fall apart to come back together from the inside out.

I met my husband right before my seventeenth birthday and we dated for a year before we got engaged. Of course I said, "yes," he was everything and, at eighteen, I could see my life laid out like a storybook.

I would be the most amazing and fulfilled homemaker, crafting with my own hands to decorate my home. I would crochet, paint cutesy wood cutouts, and learn to sew, quilt, and process my own food. My house would always be clean and tidy because I'd make sure it was all picked up every night before bed, and first thing in the morning I would run the vacuum and do a quick wipe down after breakfast.

I also knew how wonderful motherhood would be. I was an awesome babysitter who had rules and loved kids. I would spend all day with my adorable offspring, doing activities and teaching them, all while keeping everything clean and helping my husband on the farm.

What I imagined wasn't too far off from my childhood experience. I did get in trouble for not putting my dirty dishes in the dishwasher, and lost count of how often I was grounded until my room was clean. If I ignored some of my chores for long enough, my mom would get fed up and do them, "because it is easier to just do it myself." Growing up, I wanted to be like my mom. In a lot of ways, I still do.

I had many examples of the kind of womanhood I dreamed of. Many of my friends also had stay-at-home moms. Those who also went out to work were just as amazing, although I did feel bad for my friends for not having the home life I had. I was surrounded by a village of mothers who loved and welcomed me.

Some of these women were also my Sunday teachers. All those lessons were loving, encouraging, constant, and consistently reinforced traditional gender roles, especially that of a woman. Having kids was how we glorified God. Raising and nurturing them was the priority.

These lessons also included keeping a clean and orderly house, providing healthy delicious, mostly homemade, meals. And making sure that I was a dutiful, loving, and supportive wife who placed the needs and dreams of my husband above mine; he was the breadwinner and provider.

This is the ideal life. This is living the dream. I was consistently taught this dream through activities as I learned to cross stitch, iron, and sew on buttons. I learned to cook different recipes and made special cookbooks in preparation for my future marriage. I created babysitting kits with simple handmade toys and games. I was taught everything I needed to become a dutiful wife, homemaker, and mother.

My friends and I were also taught well-thought-out 'youth lessons' about staying pure. A rose was passed around the room; all the girls were told to smell it, touch it, and take a petal if we wanted to.

After it made its pass around the room, we were compared to this 'handled' rose. Our worth, value, and desirability for marriage to a 'good and honorable man' would be diminished if we gave too many kisses, or allowed ourselves to be touched too much, or in the 'wrong' places. We even had men come and tell us how to dress and behave to be considered appropriate.

We were also told to make sure our clothing didn't turn us into 'walking pornography.' Tank tops, crop tops, short shorts, and mini skirts were not allowed, and we had to keep that cleavage fully covered. Pretty much anything in the store needed to be altered with some kind of cap-sleeved undershirt that was long enough to pull down. Boys' and men's shorts were the correct length.

My worth depended upon what I wore—and what men and boys thought of it.

These lessons were to help prepare me. To protect me from being attacked by not wearing the wrong clothes, and to help me see how I could help men and boys behave properly according to the plan they were being taught. To help me marry the right man for the plan.

Well-trained for this ideal domestic, submissive life, I saw it lived out in front of me for my whole existence in the smiles and soft voices of women I loved and respected through their love and nurturing of me.

I almost pitied those girls who didn't fit perfectly into the puzzle. Even though I was told I would never *be* perfect, I was taught to always strive for perfection. I didn't judge these women; life and no one is perfect and I had every intention of doing it exactly as I had been taught.

The plan was wedded bliss, to endure and sweetly grow old together, having my posterity lauded and to be praised as I sacrificed myself for the family legacy.

Although I don't mean to, I think I may be coming across a bit snarky. I am still in the throes of processing and releasing the trauma of this betrayal. A betrayal of women sacrificing each other to maintain safety and security. Following the program and teaching it to each other over and over, or face the fear of rejection and loss.

I do believe some women can live this 'ideal' and love it. They can thrive if they clearly see all the options laid before them and truly get to choose this life. But this is different from being programmed for it, and trying to make yourself fit into it when you are not meant to. From being conditioned that it is the only way to be happy.

For decades I shut down, stuffed away, and blocked almost everything that made me, me. During my healing journey, I have been learning to love that little girl and teenager who wanted to believe some things differently. Who wanted to do some things differently. Looking back, those 'things' were normal, mesmerizing, creative, and instinctual desires.

I have realized that I did the same thing to my daughter. I taught her what I was taught, and took her regularly to learn the same lessons I learned from the same kind of women. She took it all in and dutifully did her part as well.

When she was seventeen, I hit my breaking point. I couldn't keep up the façade any longer. It was killing me, and my mental health deteriorated to the point that something needed to change or I would literally die. My daughter was at the stage of figuring out who she was going to be.

As she stepped back and took control of her own story and life, it seemed to give me the permission that I hadn't been able to give myself. I couldn't betray us both any longer, so I let go. As I let go of my need to keep her in the 'plan,' I also let go of keeping myself that way. The more free she became, the more free I became too—and we could actually see each other.

I was betrayed by a cycle in a system, and also betrayed myself, for too long.

For years, I watched other women stand up and say that it wasn't ok to continue the way we had been conditioned to, that we were being hurt. I saw those women be dismissed and quieted, then forgotten, as work to keep the status quo moved on. It was effective to keep me, and any others, silent.

During the past few years, I have had to relearn to trust my intuition and the gifts I gave up to fit in and be 'proper.' There is still a lot of work to do. I love therapy. I have started to do the activities I loved as a little girl, and my inner child is growing up with me. Some days feel heavy with a lot to process; other days I embrace being carefree.

Learning to have boundaries has been a challenge, and I have learned to notice my anger as a signpost, to see what boundary is needed. I have learned to acknowledge my parts and validate my own experience. I get to check in with myself and see what I need and I get to meet myself where I am.

I finally get to love myself for who I am.

8

MY LIFE-SAVING LESSONS OF SELF-BETRAYAL

CHRISTINE FREY

I BETRAYED MYSELF WHEN I didn't report my lifelong repeated abuse to the police. I betrayed myself when I said "yes" and "no," despite what I intuitively knew was not healthy and safe for me.

When I was fifteen, a friend came over while I was babysitting and attempted to sexually assault me. I fought him off fiercely, pushed him out the front door, and later told his girlfriend—who didn't believe me. He tried to apologize a few times, and she finally apologized when she caught him sexually assaulting someone else, but I never reported this event to anyone who could have helped me. I let myself down again.

Stuck in desperate fear of my husband cheating on me (again) and leaving me, I had a forced abortion when he threatened to kick me out of the house. This event always haunts me. I betrayed myself once again when

I didn't ask for help from someone who could have helped me prevent this shameful tragedy.

I betrayed myself twice when I was very close to death by strangulation, yet didn't tell anyone. I betrayed myself when I hid in a bush late at night, holding my two small children while watching my husband's headlights search the dark as he looked for us after he beat me in front of them. We huddled there, and when my friend arrived to pick us up, I chose to not do the right thing for myself and my children. I never reported this to the authorities, and when he apologized, I went back to him.

I betrayed myself after my drunk husband blacked out and beat me within an inch of my life. He was in a violent bar fight and, after being hit over the head, knocked out for a few seconds, and left alone on the sidewalk, he realized that someone had stolen his car keys, money, and drugs.

When he got home, he staggered in the front door to see a dark shape in the hallway. That dark shape was me. It seemed to take forever to get him to realize that the person screaming at him to stop was me begging for my life, not the guy he had argued with at the bar. He later said that he was, "hitting me like a man because he was so angry," and that his blackout began to fade when I started to quiet down while he was punching me and I was begging for my life.

Not listening to my intuition and feeling 'comfortable' with these dangerous repetitive cycles caused me to ignore my most basic needs of self-care, self-respect, and personal safety. Immersed in self-doubt, victimhood, fear, and abandonment made me feel as if I wasn't worthy, or capable of helping myself begin to thrive, not merely survive.

While my children were toddlers, I worked full-time in a gym I loved and attended college part-time to pursue a degree in physical education. It was a challenge to go to college because my husband was envious of the time I spent away from home. I either organized babysitters or took my children to school with me because, many times, my husband was drunk before he got home or didn't come home to watch them.

He was angry when I tried to do my homework because he saw it as wasted time and an attempt to better myself and leave him. Once, he hid my school books, so I had to hide them from him after that. He also tried to block my car in the driveway so I couldn't leave, which caused me to drive across the lawn and, one time, he punched out all the lightbulbs in the house so I couldn't study and write reports. I did graduate with my associate's degree and wanted to pursue my bachelor's, but the violence at home escalated.

I used to consider self-betrayal and self-abandonment as tools for survival and as essential components of my life. These destructive and unhealthy behaviors were instinctively learned during my childhood; they were so ingrained in my spirit, body, mind, and emotions that I thought they were always going to be an essential part of my existence.

Feeling fearful and embarrassed about the alcoholism, bruises, and constant violence in my home and relationships was pervasive. That young girl only knew strife, struggle, and scarcity-consciousness; her life had to be difficult and scary. She intuitively knew how to keep dirty secrets and to 'numb out' and disassociate to protect herself.

Learning how to read people's body language and energy gave her a heads up as to whether she needed to talk calmly and distract them from the dangerous situation, or to hide and not be seen. This also helped her to figure out what her next right step should be—should she stay or run and hide?

I truly believed it when I told myself that I stayed in unhealthy relation-ships to prove that I was stronger and better off than my parents but, in truth, I was not ok.

My husband died from alcoholism and substance abuse when I was forty-nine years old. That's when my healing journey began. I realized that I had never been my own friend but I felt indifferent to that thought It was so easy to be kind to other people, to give them everything that I thought I didn't deserve and couldn't give—didn't give—myself.

Thinking I was worthy, enough, and deserving felt incomprehensible and foreign. *Who was I to think I deserved respect, love, kindness, grace, honesty, and compassion when I didn't feel those things for myself?* I saw no need to treat myself more kindly than I had been treated because I deeply believed that I was not worthy.

Staying in unhealthy relationships caused me to continue to sell myself short, and to firmly believe that I wasn't enough and would never have enough. Tolerating poor treatment while wallowing in the struggle of fear, abuse, and dysfunction was where I felt most comfortable because it was all I knew. I did reach out for help a few times, yet I never fully committed to saving myself because the struggle to do so felt too difficult and overwhelming.

Surviving my destructive childhood and subsequent violent marriages made me think I didn't have a way out, or even that I wanted a way out. The audacity to ask for help and safety was beyond my realm of comprehension and I was way too tired to fight for myself. *Who was I to think I deserved better?*

I truly perceived that my life was always going to be the struggle I had always known, and that my unhealed self and poor choices were the accepted consequences. To be honest, I continually lied to myself, took no responsibility for my actions and lack of actions, and pretended to be someone other than my authentic self.

When I was twenty-nine, I received my last beating from my husband, then quickly started dating, and subsequently married my next abusive husband. When I was thirty-two years old, I received a pacemaker to calm my extra heartbeats and low blood pressure. The pacemaker was required to calm my autonomic nervous system because my 'fight, flight, freeze, and fawn' reaction was stuck on overdrive. I had extra heart beats and a very low pulse from the persistent abuse that wrecked my autonomic nervous system.

With no awareness of how these acts of self-betrayal felt to me, I was so disconnected from myself that I didn't trust myself to know what was best for me.

Trauma and self-betrayal are very deeply connected. I had no idea that I was stuck in this cycle of trauma and self-betrayal, and that my tendency to minimize my own needs, play small, not cause any trouble, and keep the peace at all costs was so destructive. Codependency was my best friend and survival buddy.

I now understand that self-betrayal is a huge component of codependency. One of the many devastating effects of living in these traumatic, neglectful, and chaotic environments was the pervasive pattern of self-betrayal and self-abandonment.

For forty-nine years, I felt like I had to prove my worth. To do this, I poured myself into someone else, making sure they got what they needed, while not receiving what I needed, wanted, or liked. I didn't trust my intuition, instincts, and the need to set boundaries, and suppressed my emotions which caused me to feel resentful and unappreciated.

I received many injuries to my body, including a claw hammer in my foot when I was twenty, and had to go to work despite the debilitating pain. I have permanent ear damage, and throat and neck trauma from repeated strangulations. While being physically abused, I learned to position my body to take the least damage and to try to hide the bruises.

Today, my strong beautiful body tells the stories I couldn't put into clear thoughts and healing words while I was stuck in the cycle of trauma and self-betrayal.

Very recently, I had a cancer health scare that involved my throat. My throat is now my most protected body part, and to have testing done in this area was scary and cathartic at the same time. While I was scared I had cancer, I was also relieved to know that I was now strong enough to ask my throat what it was trying to teach me. My throat was showing me that it's ok to make noise, speak up for myself with ease, express myself freely, creatively, and joyously, and be willing to change.

Wow! This was everything I never thought I deserved, desired, or would acquire, and it is everything I am now actively working for in my life. On this realization, I immediately reached out with humility and honesty to my prayer friends to tell them that this was probably caused by my earlier self-betrayal and trauma.

Asking for help is something I am working on as it was not something I was accustomed to doing. I always thought I was a 'tough girl' who didn't need help; in reality, I was afraid that if I asked for help I would be perceived as weak, needy, or not worthy. I continued to pray for the wisdom to learn the valuable lessons my throat was trying to teach me so I could honor my soul and follow the path that God set before me.

I now see the value in both myself and the practice of self-forgiveness as I learn why I chose the life-saving choices I made to survive and betray myself at the same time. Through therapy I have learned why I repeatedly engaged in unhealthy and dangerous relationships while desiring to give my precious children a better life. I love my children more than anyone and anything, and I needed them to show me that life can be beautiful, good, and full of love.

Living the way we did was not healthy for them, and I didn't realize that the extent of the trauma and damage they were exposed to continued to perpetuate the cycle of violence I was raised in. My children and I are survivors and I am beyond grateful that we are now thriving and on the other side of our trauma cycles. I firmly believed that my life was supposed to be a dangerous struggle, and that's why I chose to silently wear my trauma as a badge of honor.

Who do I think I am and how dare I speak up now? Well, my dear, I am thriving! I am still adjusting to the knowledge that I am safe, loved, respected, and enough, because the survivor mindset is still ingrained in my mind, body and emotions. There are still many times when I find it difficult to understand why I now have love, beauty, peace, ease, calm, and potentiality in my life.

I am truly grateful. I sing with joy that I am alive to experience the amazing adventures and opportunities that God presents to me. People have asked me why I prayed to God when it appeared that he was silent, and I gladly told them that I stood in my own way time and time again. He was always with me but I didn't befriend Him because I was not healthy and ready to let go of my struggles.

It is so much easier to hold onto what's not serving you when it's all you know. With my spiritual work, however, I have learned that it takes much more effort to release all that was holding me back. I still feel the subconscious effects of my self-betrayal and self-abandonment, and I have learned to recognize this when I easily fly off the handle, overreact, take things personally, over-eat, and feel deep anxiety.

Through my Shamanic work, faith, therapy, and other healing modalities, I now have healthy tools in my emotional toolbox. Surrounding myself with safe, emotionally mature people, creating firm healthy boundaries, knowing that the word 'no' is a complete sentence, and being fully present in my body are some of my healthy tools.

Asking for help and receiving help are two powerful gifts I have ingrained in my life, even though these are not things I would have ever considered for myself. Pausing before I speak, feeling my breath in my body, grounding and connecting to my Higher Power and spiritual support team are fantastic tools that help me feel safe and surrounded by those who love me.

I am a beautiful "work in progress," and I would never change anything about my life because I have had the blessing to learn so many soul lessons in such a short amount of time. If I am lucky, I will live to be one-hundred years old, and that's only a blip on the radar as far as lifetimes go. This is a powerful lifetime for me because I have grown and evolved as a chainbreaker, feeling and healing my emotions so I can honor my soul. I am honest about my life because I hope to inspire and empower someone else who feels lost, unworthy, alone, and without a voice.

My work as a Shamanic healer enables me to help people reclaim their personal power, find their authentic voice, begin their transformative healing journey, and heal spiritually, mentally, emotionally, and physically.

My beautiful journey has taught me to trust, grow, release my pain, and learn more about myself than I ever imagined! I am a soul living in the human body I deliberately chose for this lifetime to pursue my soul purposes. In my human body, my soul is having a human experience and I know that the more I purposefully walk my spiritual path, the more I honor my sweet soul.

My journey is far from over and I can't wait to see what I discover about myself, those around me, and the healing possibilities we all have available to us. We need to have faith, trust, and the belief in our innate ability to heal ourselves while learning who we truly are as a soul.

Thank you for reading my story and I wish you many blessings, peace, and love.

9

THE LADY WITHIN

TERI KATZENBERGER

A s I SIT DOWN to write my part of this anointed book, I can't help but wonder, *What is this thing called Life really about?*

You see, I have been asking myself this question for most of my time here on Earth. Maybe I came into this world with too high expectations and grand assumptions about what life would be like. I mean, I was born into a family with two parents, an older brother and sister, and a fabulous twin brother! Isn't it simply a given to expect love, respect, kindness, compassion, nurture, attention, and appreciation; *a family?*

When you are born into a home that doesn't welcome you nor want you—into a family where you don't fit in—how do you grow up to feel and believe you will fit in *anywhere else*, outside those four walls?

In January 1968, my twin brother and I became the greatest upset to ever happen. We ruined our mother's life!

I ponder: *be·trayed: treacherously abandoned, deserted, or mistreated. To be hurt, broken. Mistreated by way of verbal, emotional and/or mental abuse.*

And so, I continue to question: *What is this all about? What am I all about? What have I become? Who have I become?* Words do not flow smoothly from my lips these days. I cannot seem to gather a thought as to how I even begin to share my story in this book about betrayal.

One day I closed my eyes, sat back, and took time to pray upon and ask the Lord to give me direction—to put my thoughts aside and allow the Holy Spirit to guide and write my words. Suddenly, it all became crystal clear. Get out of my head and into my heart!

Allow me to introduce myself: *My Name is be·trayed: treacherously abandoned, deserted, or mistreated. To be hurt, broken. Mistreated by way of verbal, emotional and/or mental abuse.*

Unwelcomed Intruder

Born Teresa Ann Thompson, my twin brother and I came into this world each weighing three pounds. Although he was able to leave the hospital soon after our birth, I remained in an incubator for the next three weeks. I was told the nurses and staff absolutely *loved* 'Baby Polly.' Yes, I was named Polly for three weeks until my dad encouraged my mother to change it, for obvious reasons—"Polly wanna cracker?"

I was born to a woman who never wanted me. She had plans of her own—for the future of herself and her first- and second-born children. Don't get me wrong, we all have the same dad and my parents were married. My mother's life, however, was not at all that she desired for herself.

The day she had planned to finally leave my dad, and take the two 'golden children' (my brother and sister) with her, was the day she found out she was pregnant—with twins! So my mother chose to stay with our father. But these are the two most important words: "She chose!" Who knows, maybe *she* felt betrayed?

On January 7, 1968, the 'Unwelcomed Intruders' were born. I grew up in a house that was divided into 'Them' against 'Us.' My mother and her two golden children against my dad and the twins. We were the Intruders in this old house and we were never able to live it down nor break away from the stigma of 'ruining my mother's life.'

As a child, your home should be a safe place. But to this Intruder, it was just a house. I was never made to feel welcome there. I lived in an angry, loud, hate-filled container, constantly hearing the words, "You make my life miserable." *How could I possibly strive to overcome that? Who was I going to become with that level of programming? How could I even begin to make sense of my existence, let alone believe that I could make my mother proud?* Nothing about me was good enough, nor would anything about me ever be good enough.

How do I know? I spent my life from birth through to December 2021 trying to capture the positive attention of my mother. If my life successes were based on that mission alone, I would die an epically-doomed failure who never amounted to anything. A lifelong unwelcome intruder who had zero hope and even less chance to make anything of her life. Another great saying that forever haunts me is, "You will never amount to anything."

The very sight of me made my mother cringe. The sound of my voice was like screeching to her ears. "Stop your screeching!" still pierces *my* ears. When people voice that I look like my dad's mother, it makes my mom's skin crawl. The very sight of me made my mom ill, angry, and feel betrayed. *Betrayed?* She forever blames me for becoming pregnant with me. The twins who destroyed her life and made her life a living hell for all the days of *our* life. Read *that* sentence again.

I have lived forever with the sense of abandonment and great loss. I was desperate, crying out to belong to a family. To *have* a family. I never fit in. I was never welcomed in. I was never made to feel anything but an intruder and life destroyer. A huge unwanted burden. The ultimate betrayal towards my mother. *Really?*

I grew up with internal thoughts and dialogue of, "This isn't a real family," "A mother doesn't treat her child this way," and, "This isn't what a marriage is." *How could a child of such a young age have such profound thoughts and feelings on life?*

Every night I cried myself to sleep as I sat at the heat vent in my room listening to the 'adults' yell and degrade each other. The mental, emotional, and verbal abuse haunts me to this day. It has caused me 17,155+ sleepless nights as I battled chronic, disabling insomnia. For some dysfunctional reason, I thought it was my right to know what the parents were fighting about. In a loud, angry, hate-filled house, I did my best to be a 'peacemaker,' to bring cheer and love to our family dynamic. But the anger was always directed at the Intruders. The hate and discontent were brought on by our very existence.

—◦✦◦—

Mission Impossible

I strived for perfection, attention, and to just be 'wanted.' I got A's and B's throughout school. Some years I achieved the 'Perfect Attendance Award,' earned other awards and ribbons, and excelled in school events and activities. But it seemed that no matter what I did or how well I did it, the 'it' would go unrecognized. How I longed to hear the words, "I am so proud of you Teri," "Way to go," and "Good Job!"

Never have I heard words of encouragement or appreciation. In high school, I was thrilled to earn a scholarship to a local college, but I was left to pat myself on the back and figure out which classes to take, even how to enroll—all on my own.

Being 'good enough' became the main mission of my young life. I set my standards low and strived to just be 'enough.' Although deep down I truly believed I was worth so much more than those around me would ever acknowledge, I did everything to hear the words, "I am so proud of you."

To see a smile on her face as she looked at me. To hear soft, kind words as she spoke to me. To have her boast to friends and relatives about my accomplishments as I grew up. But, since I wasn't one of the 'golden children,' it really didn't matter what I did. I did it as a silent intruder.

Little did I know that my life's—self-image-damaging—mission would remain *impossible* in all senses of the word. I was never prepared to grow up a dysfunctional perfectionist who never knew what it felt like to simply be happy! All I wanted was a family who loved me and to be happy in this thing called life 'My Life.'

Honestly, to this very day, I have lived my life believing that this is not too much to ask. If my life successes were based on that mission alone, I would die an epically-doomed failure who never amounted to anything. A life-long unwelcome intruder who had zero hope and even less chance to make anything of her life.

Polly: The Lady Within

What if Polly lives in me? What if she *is* me and I *am* her? What if she is the person who has been my strength, my confidence, my determination—The Lady Within? My hope and desire to live life out loud?

If not for the Lady Within, I would never have had the strength and grace to survive a lifetime of verbal, mental, and emotional abuse at the hands of my mother.

You see, the Lady Within clashed with my mother. She stood up for what was right. She always had a voice. I didn't conform to my mother's world and her views. I wasn't a naughty child. I never disrespected her. I had a voice and she despised that. Always has, always will.

The Lady Within stood tall, kept her grace, and loved her family anyway. You see, I could have gone through life forever having the thoughts, words, and opinions of others hold me back and chain me down. Instead, I continued to be me and go out into the world as God Created me.

I was born *to* my parents, I was not born *of them*.

Betrayed NOT Broken

Betrayed: The Sister Wounds that broke our hearts, but transformed into opportunities for health, growth, and abundance!

What is this thing called Life really about? As I lay at the feet of Jesus allowing the Holy Spirit to speak to me, it was revealed loud and clear!

Life isn't about me at all! I was flooded with memories of mentors, people who have sown great words of wisdom throughout my life.

Back in 2004, a mentor told me, "It's not about you." In response, I thought, *The heck if it's not!* Although I was just being funny, in reality, I didn't understand what he meant. All I knew was that those words would remain forever in my consciousness. He never explained to my business partner and me what he meant; he left us to, "figure it out and let me know when you do."

It wasn't until a couple of years later that it really hit me: "It's *not* about *me*." When I took myself out of the equation, I began to realize that all that goes on in the world around me isn't about me at all. I began to realize that the way people feel about me and act towards me, isn't about me, Teresa Ann Thompson. It's about them, and to remain in my dysfunction would be to continue to make all things about me. I discovered that I don't need to take on the weight of another person's world!

We were at a family gathering at my sister's house when I finally set myself free from the verbal, mental, and emotional abuse of my mother. Once again, she began to belittle me in front of my sister, older brother, and their families. I couldn't defend myself enough from her words as she recalled something 'completely embarrassing' that had happened at an event I attended with my sister and her.

I continued to stand my ground, telling her, "I have no idea what you are talking about. That wasn't me."

She insisted that it was and added, "Didn't you just feel absolutely stupid by acting that way in front of_____?"

I continued to respond, "Mother, that was *not* me. I did not say that. I did not do that. I have no clue what you are talking about."

We batted the belittling back and forth as I continued to receive her words, "Don't you feel so stupid. How could you not have felt so stupid. You looked so stupid!"

Then I heard a soft voice and a chuckle as my sister confessed, "Mom, that was me. I said that to_____."

And the two of them laughed and laughed. It's like a knife to my heart when my mother, sister, and older brother laugh at me. They belittle me, make me the butt of jokes, and cause me to feel and look 'stupid' purely so they can laugh *at* me.

On this particular day I kindly asked my mother, "Why is it that every time you think about something stupid someone has done, you automatically think of me?" She just chuckled and snickered, along with my sister. No belittling of my sister. No telling my sister how stupid she looked. No letting my sister know how gravely she had embarrassed my mother at the event.

In contrast, my mother continually gets joy out of verbally beating me by bringing up things from ten, twenty, even thirty, years ago.

If there was a hole in the earth during this conversation, I would have welcomed falling into it and disappearing forever. Instead, I got up, went into the house to 'get water,' then walked out the front door, got in my car, and drove away. As I turned the corner, the tears fell from my eyes like a tidal wave. I couldn't control my reaction; shaking so hard, for a moment, I thought I would have to pull over. At that very moment I had become absolutely broken.

On that winding ride home, I cried out to the Lord, "Why? Why do they treat me the way they do? What is it about me that makes them treat me this way?"

My Heavenly Father answered me by simply saying, "Forgive them for they know not *what* they say. They know not *how* they make you feel. They know not *what* they do." At this exact moment, when I received God's word and repeated it out loud, forty-three years of pain, sadness, sorrow, and loneliness were removed.

And so the story goes, "It's not about you!"

Step out of what is forever haunting you and causing you anguish and inner torment and say out loud, 'It's not about me!' Dear beautiful sister —yes, you reading this book—it is 100,000% OK to set yourself free. I am giving you permission right here and right now. Get Up! And go 'get a water!'

Breaking Through

Once you sit back and begin to reflect on all aspects of your life—the good, the bad, and the ugly—you will be amazed at all the *good* you have experienced, particularly in regard to people.

On April 9, 2022, another mentor (who I still know today) taught me a *huge* lesson at a Business Conference shared with a few hundred colleagues from across the world. During certain times throughout our conference, we could go up to the microphone to share a 'takeaway,' an 'A-ha!' moment, a business tip, whatever we felt called to speak about.

During the four days, most people told a story about their childhood or upbringing as they reached breakthroughs they were not expecting. At times it appeared fitting and understandable why some would share their personal backstories.

On day three, when asked, "for those to come up to share what break-through or experience they just had from our last segment," I got up to share. There were probably fifteen people ahead of me, so it took a couple of hours before I made it to the microphone. Interestingly, the voice in my head kept telling me to sit down but I continued to wait my turn. Go figure?

And then it was my turn! I shared that my breakthrough was such an eye-opener, and began to tell my 'story' from the day I was born through childhood. I explained that I never felt loved by my family, nor did I grow up in a loving home. I talked about my mother and how I completely disrupted her life, making it a forever living hell.

Five minutes into my share, just as I was on the verge of explaining my eye-opening breakthrough, the leader said from the stage, "Yeah. Yeah. Yeah, Teri. Your mother sounds like a horrible person. Did you have a breakthrough? Get to the breakthrough."

Instantly crushed, my heart sank. My mind went blank. He completely disrupted my state. It was his tone, his sense of disgust. Just as I was about to get to my breakthrough, he disrupted my flow. There I stood. Blank. Embarrassed. Crushed. Why? Now it all seems so foolish, but the fifteen-plus people who had gone before me spoke for fifteen-to-twenty minutes each. During their speeches, the leader was calm, listened, and allowed them to share themselves openly and freely.

I never did share my breakthrough at the mic. I was so caught off guard that, again, if there was a hole in the earth, I would have welcomed falling into it and forever disappearing from this thing called 'My Life.' I simply said, "Um......I realized I was born with overwhelming love in my heart, yet I have never felt love." And I sat down. I could not wait for the day to end. When it did, I went back to my hotel room and cried my eyes out.

It was so interesting that his words alone bothered me way more than his actions. I cried. I prayed. I reached out to a close friend and felt some level of sanity return when she said she was shocked at how he treated me from the stage. She said, "The look on your face said it all. I knew immediately that he caught you off guard and deeply hurt you."

My emotions from his tone and words were so disabling that I almost left and hopped on a plane that night! I barely slept. His words continued to roll through my head like a bad audio tape. And then it hit me! That voice. That tone. It was as if my mother was talking through him. I heard *her* voice. *Her* tone. I thought I was going to be sick. Instead, I had an amazing—and freeing—breakthrough.

You see, all of my life I have felt invisible. I have always felt like there is absolutely nothing about me or my life that matters to anyone, especially my family. They have never been interested in anything about my life. They don't care to visit with me; they never have.

I began to be flooded with my mother's words, "Stop your screeching," "You will never amount to anything," "You make my life miserable." But it's not just the words, it's the tone. That tone is like a bad record that haunts my mind.

This 'breakthrough from the breakthrough' made me realize that I have been a silent intruder in this thing called 'My Life.' The *abrupt disrupter* (my mentor) triggered emotions that I was not at all prepared for. He made me realize that, although my emotions and my 'story' may be triggered by people, places, and things, it does not mean that it is my truth or my reality. Instead, it remains the great reminder: "It is not about you!" When I realized why I was so broken after that particular moment at our conference, it felt like a thousand-pound weight was lifted from my shoulders.

I won't lie or candy-coat it. The next day at the conference I had to use all my willpower not to take back all I had let go of during the night. I had to be mindful of my own thoughts and words so I did not disrupt those triggers. *How did I do that?* By not talking about it. I did not bring attention to it. I had let it go and I intended to let it be gone! You see, as easy as we, 'let it go,' we can just as easily 'take it back!' You may wonder why this is such a big deal to me.

Before I left for this conference, I prayed for specific things. First of all, I was in the process of overcoming disabling anxiety, social anxiety, and depression.

During 2020 and through to 2022, I had become a broken introvert almost afraid of my own shadow. I had once been a social butterfly, always out and about in the community and with people. But, you know what those two years brought us and there is no need to say any more. All I can say is that I survived my suicidal thoughts, even while watching my in-person business be destroyed and disappear.

Making the decision to attend this live conference was a huge step for me. However, I had made the conscious decision in January 2022 that I was going to take my life back! So before I left for this conference, I prayed for: laser focus, clear vision, and clarity for my future. I prayed to have ears to hear the truth, eyes to see what was real, and a heart to receive. I hopped on the plane to Texas with zero expectations and only the certainty that I would receive what was meant for me.

Day four arrived and my mentor said (from the stage) that we all reach a time when we need to get past our story. He said (and I am not quoting verbatim), "So many of you come up and start with your story. I acknowledge all of you who were vulnerable to share things with strangers in this room that some of your friends may not even know about. Let's leave it all here. Use your story as your motivator. There comes a time when we no longer have to tell our 'story' to move forward, especially if it sets you back instead of moving you forward."

Here's the real, raw, truth—this hit me! I felt another thousand-pound weight lift as I found myself letting out a huge sigh of release. Not relief. *Release!* He was spot on. It was then that I realized I need to close the final chapter on my 'Before Story' and begin to write a brand new one with focus, vision, and clarity for a bright new future. For this thing called 'My Life!'

My past does *not* equal my future. I am a victor, *not* a victim. From that moment forward, I realized the most important thing is what I have learned from my 'Before Story.' Now I can successfully begin to touch and change lives with my 'After Story.' The story of a divine overcomer. The story of a woman who was betrayed but *not* broken.

Beautifully Wounded and Set Free

As a wounded sister, if you can remove yourself from the attitudes, opinions, and actions of others, you can ultimately set yourself free to heal and to grow. You no longer need to wear the heavy cloak called: *be·trayed: treacherously abandoned, deserted, or mistreated. To be hurt, broken. Mistreated by way of verbal, emotional and/or mental abuse.*

I walked away from that conference a woman who armed herself with strength, confidence, and determination to continue to break through the impossible! Our 'Before Story' is a deeply significant part of us. It may even be who we became. Never deny that. However, our 'Before Story' is not *who* we are. It is with this book, this chapter—right here, right now—that I encourage you to, "Get up and go get a water!" Then reach out and allow me to help you begin your 'After Story.'

You may be wondering about my eye-opening breakthrough. It was: God created me for one reason—to walk in peace, to love and serve His people. When I was born, He filled my heart with *all* the love that was poured into that 'old house.' The Twins soaked up all of God's Love. We received it.

Yet we went through every waking day not ever knowing what it really felt like to be loved. We may never know what it means to receive Love. However, we lived every moment of our days loving, giving to, walking with, and standing by other people. Lifting others up and letting them know they are loved and that they matter!

My twin passed away very unexpectedly on December 9, 2020. Half of me has gone to heaven while the other half remains here on earth, continuing to fight for this thing called 'Our Life.' Today our 'After Story' begins.

When you have been wounded, broken, betrayed, abandoned, and just forgotten, you can either accept the world's view of you, or trust the voice in your heart that continues to remind you, "You are so much more than you think you are!"

This reminds me of one of my very first 'silent' mentors. Back in 2000, I watched his teachings, leaned on every word, and was forever changed when he said, "You are so much more than you think you are!" Then he'd say, "Repeat after me—*louder*—*You are so much more than you think you are!*"

Every day since, I have shouted those words over, and over, and over. I have passed that uplifting message of positive hope to thousands of people over the years. I still do so today.

I say 'silent mentor' because, at a business conference I attended in May 2000, I was expecting to meet this amazing, handsome man who had a profound impact on my life. Although I watched many videos, teachings, and tapings of his, I had yet to meet him in person. You can imagine my devastation when, at the conference, we received the news that he had passed away. I was at a loss for words. Numb. Lost

When the organizers put a video up on the big screen with a message he had previously recorded, I heard his voice and those words, "You are so much more than you think you are!" It was then that I fully understood and believed that there *are* Angels amongst us.

During the coming years, I truly came to understand that the family I was born into are not my people. I was merely an unwelcomed intruder born into a house without a home. A dynamic of individuals without a family. I may never know what it's like to actually have a family. I may never know what 'family' really means. or what it truly is.

But I do know, for certain, that family is not: *be·trayed: treacherously abandoned, deserted, or mistreated. To be hurt, broken. Mistreated by way of verbal, emotional and/or mental abuse.*

In 1996, I learned that the people you love deeply may never feel the same for you as you do for them. They may never have love in their heart the way you do for them. They may never think about you the way you think about them. Most individuals probably never experienced a fifth of what I have been through in my life. Learning the cold, hard truth about my mother and my family was still the most painful breakthrough of my life.

I remember the moment I awakened to this damaging truth: Family may not think of you as you do them. They may not love you as you love them. I remember the pain as if it was yesterday. I truly thought it would be the one thing that completely broke me, especially when the people who hurt me were my family.

In April 1991, at twenty-three years old, I overcame a grossly abusive marriage, a chronic, life-threatening alcohol and drug addiction, and a chronic dual-health-damaging eating disorder.

And by God's Grace, I was set free from spending two-to-four years in a women's prison. However, *nothing could* have prepared me for the pain I endured from learning the truth about, "people may never feel for you / love you / think about you, the way you do them."

No matter how painful it was, the one thing that truly set me free from this reality was when I openly spoke those words out loud, admitted the truth behind them, and accepted that truth.

You see, that is the part of my 'Before Story' that never goes away. However, I can choose to 'live in it,' or I can choose to 'move out of it.' In 1996, I moved out of it!

Every waking day I choose to give thanks for my family. I choose to Thank God for watching over my family, keeping them safe, and protecting them from all harm. I continue to Thank Him for keeping them healthy, well, fit, strong, and whole. I CHOOSE LOVE!

So, The Story Goes

"For God so loved the world that he gave his one and only Son, that whoever believes in him shall not perish but have eternal life."

John 3:16

"For I know the plans I have for you," declares the LORD, "plans to prosper you and not to harm you, plans to give you hope and a future."

Jeremiah 29:11

I *choose* to Believe and to live *My Life* out loud! Free to be unapologetically me—Teresa A Thompson, Polly, The Lady Within! I *choose* to have hope and a bright future. To prosper and live in my divine destiny here on earth.

I dedicate my story to my handsome father and my fabulous twin brother. Although I miss them every waking day, I remain forever blessed and thankful they are living their best life with their Supernatural Anointed Father and their divine family in heaven.

IO

I FEAR THE MANY FACES

HELEN STAINES

I fear the many faces, many personalities in me. Sometimes I fail to understand my self and become deceived by my various selves.

Ama H. Vanniarachchy

I UNDERSTAND BETRAYAL. IT has happened countless times throughout my life, from experiencing sexual abuse as an innocent nine-year-old (by a trusted neighbour who highly betrayed that trust), to the alcohol abuse and domestic violence perpetrated by my second husband during our marriage, and the terror he imposed on my children and myself when I ended our relationship.

To say life has been a journey of ups and downs, of small and large betrayals, sums it up perfectly. Perhaps it has even been a learning journey.

When I deeply examine my life, I have to admit that the biggest and longest-lasting betrayal of all is my betrayal of Self.

The years of joy and freedom lost from being in a body I loathed. Decades of battling low self-esteem because I didn't—couldn't—accept and love who I was. I never gave myself the compassion and forgiveness I so easily show other people. For decades I was my biggest critic, fueled by my previous husbands who found fault in my weight and size, not to mention the consuming and incessant media and advertising that constantly reminded me I was not enough.

I now believe a factor that initially contributed to my body issues and low self-esteem was the trauma of being sexually abused so young. I was a nine-year-old girl lured into acts that no child should have to do, and still remember everything so vividly.

The warm summer night. The colour of the summer pajamas I wore. The TV show that was playing at the time. The touch of his rough hands on my innocent body, and the horrendous acts that followed. The depth of despair and confusion I felt when I was dismissed back to bed was too much for me to deal with; such embarrassment and shame, and so much guilt. It wasn't my fault, but his. He should have been embarrassed but when I saw him the very next day, he just smiled at me.

I carried his shame and guilt for decades. Such deep betrayal, so much damage inflicted, so many tears I cried for the child of Self. So many tears I cried that no one ever saved me.

I suspect this abuse may have led to two marriages where I was not my authentic self, and which both had toxic traits. My coping mechanisms attracted toxic relationships and narcissistic people, and I was the ultimate 'people-pleaser' who tried to maintain a peaceful relationship at all costs—well, at all costs to my authentic self.

During these past few years, I have come a long way, although some days I still struggle and slip back into old habits, behaviours, and thoughts. It is so hard to break the cycle of years of conditioning and coping mechanisms, but the love of a good man—my third and final husband, the lid to my pot, the missing piece to my puzzle—has allowed me to see my worth. Unbeknown to him, he has helped significantly on my journey to finding a level of peace and acceptance with myself. I am healing and it is a very good feeling.

In my late teens, I developed disordered eating, mainly in the form of Bulimia and skipping meals. Fueled by my own internal belief that I was not good enough and the pressure from my then-husband to conform to a small size, I began a love-hate relationship with my eating disorder that has been exhausting and suffocating for as long as I can remember.

Good days, bad days; my life was, and still is, a roller coaster. Accompanied by guilt and the constant worry of how I perceive that others see my Self, my toxic shame was so overwhelming and uncomfortable that it led to a secondary battle with Anxiety. For so long I felt broken and flawed—no one could possibly understand and still love me.

The embarrassment, guilt, and shame of not being strong enough to resist the urge to succumb to my eating disorder. time and time again, held me back from sharing my struggles with my high school friends and first husband. Eating disorders were shamed upon and joked about, and I remember the comments my friends and husband would make about them.

How could I possibly share my struggles with a man who should protect and love me, when I believed all he would do was tell me to, "just stop" and laugh at me? So I stayed quiet until I was in my early twenties.

Even now, I vividly remember confiding in my best friend at the time. I thought I could count on her support but I was so wrong. She judged, she didn't understand, and from that moment on I vowed to never tell anyone of my daily struggles with my body image. I allowed myself to believe that no one would understand, so I fiercely protected myself by hiding my eating disorder and the shame that came with it.

One of my biggest betrayals to Self is that I suffered in silence, alone. I wish I hadn't believed that I couldn't trust anyone; I wish I had been brave enough to try and seek help.

After decades of trying to be stronger than I felt, I finally decided it was time to reach out and be embraced for who I really am. I chose my sister because we were close. She had earned the right to hear my truth and deserved to see my most authentic Self. She listened, showed me compassion, and didn't judge me at all. The love and bond between us remained, perhaps stronger than ever. I took a chance and I was loved just the same way. I didn't feel flawed or like a freak; I was just me.

Taryn Brumfit, Australian of the year, body positivity advocate, writer, photographer, filmmaker, and founder of the *Body Image Movement* wisely said, *"It is not our life's purpose to be at war with our body,"* but war with my body feels all too natural; it seems to be my base normal.

Now, I realise that I am truly blessed by the peace found only in the intimate moments with my beloved husband. Moments where we seem to merge as one and the entire world ceases to exist, when it is only him and me and the bond of love that we share for each other. These moments are magic and I have never shared them with anyone else. Gone are the worries of my body not fitting the stereotype. Gone are the worries of tummy rolls and jiggly bits. All that exists is the two of us and the incredible power of love and acceptance.

The bubble of peace and tranquility lasts for a while after we transcend time and place into our beautiful world of blissful happiness. It exists as a calm acceptance with Self, no negative thoughts, no loathing or hatred for my self-defined inadequacies. There is no safer place felt than in the protective arms of my hubby, embraced lovingly, his hands tracing over my soft body and curves, his actions demonstrating his love and acceptance of me just as I am.

There are still some emotional triggers that I can't shake. Some wait for me in darkness; it's unknown to me how I will react. A chain reaction of emotions that can harm me and revive feelings of inadequacy. Spiraling down the black hole of despair, I want to stop hurting. The endless, overwhelming self-loathing takes over. The misery returns.

The department store fitting rooms were once a place of happiness in my youth. Endless shopping trips trying on clothes with friends. So much laughter, so much fun. But they changed over time and lost their appeal.

I have now lost count of the number of times I have walked out of a changeroom feeling defeated, sad, and unworthy of love. All those mirrors, the angles, and lighting—when will they make a change room that is flattering? And the sizing of clothing is so different from brand to brand. Sometimes even within a brand there can be mind-boggling differences.

I know I am not alone in my frustration. When buying new clothes, I feel betrayed that my body doesn't fit the 'normal' mold and standard. Anger fills me that the joy of buying new clothes has escaped me, forever out of my grasp.

The bathroom: most days I undress, unlovingly grab at my tummy, and think, *One day I will be slim again.* Full of resentment for my imperfect body, I enter the shower and wish my days away, days until I may be skinny again. Gratitude fills me as I step out of the shower and can't see my reflection in the steamed-up mirror. I dress and don't clear the fog until my body is hidden.

But there are rare days when I am strong of mind. While naked, I stand in front of the mirror and practice gratitude. My eyes, I truly love them. Such depths of beautiful blue, like an ocean shining with the ray of the sun, varying with my mood and the colour of my clothes. My smile. One of the things my hubby loves about me. My ample breasts. Yes, hubby loves these too! My beautiful tattoos, such detailed works of art. The stretch marks and scar that two pregnancies have left behind. The tummy overhang, or 'mummy pooch,' that has increased with age and is, again, the result of pregnancy.

I try desperately to remind myself that my body was, and still is, amazing. It has created two beautiful children. It is strong. It is mostly healthy. It is perfectly imperfect. I try to believe—although most days it is difficult.

There is not a time that bathroom scales have not been part of my life. The morning ritual of standing on the scales to weigh myself dictated how my day would start. Self-praise or disgust. So often I feel betrayed by myself; betrayed that I am not strong enough to resist the temptation of yummy food, not strong enough or disciplined enough to exercise more or go to the gym.

Once though, I ditched the scales. Locked them in the shed. Laugh as you may, it felt good to remove them from the bathroom and the temptation. For the short time it lasted, I felt a sense of freedom. A sense of not being a slave to the scales or social norms. But I soon slipped back into old habits, and they now sit again in my bathroom, greeting me each morning with a sinister smile.

Let's be truthful, the suitcases of 'clothes I will one day fit into,' aka 'the skinny clothes'—I know I am not alone in this guilty secret! Three suitcases and countless bags stashed away in my wardrobe. These are the clothes I am holding onto in the hope that I may one day fit into them, because I keep telling myself that I am not going to be this size forever, right?

Is it the guilt of the money spent and, therefore, lost? Or the delusion that I may one day drop four clothing sizes? My mind is in a constant state of, 'this size is temporary,' it's a constant project of trying to reach the magical smaller size that will make me feel whole and worthy. This project is now entering its thirty-second year. No size I have been is ever small enough to satisfy the self-perception of perfection.

Am I ready to throw out those hidden clothes? Maybe soon, but I praise the small steps in acknowledging the truth that one day they must go.

At some point during the last few years, something changed in me. I decided it was time to start to take responsibility for myself, to begin the healing process of changing the dysfunctional repetitive patterns in my life. Although it is difficult at times, I am proud of my journey as I began courageously to look inside myself, examine my triggers and question my very being, beliefs, thoughts, and actions. What a journey this was and still is; I have achieved so much but there is still such a long way to go.

My trauma that I have carried over the years has been acknowledged and worked through with a psychologist. It was a difficult and emotional process, but necessary. I faced my demons and I can finally tell my story out loud. There is no shame or guilt left on my part. The guilt is owned by the man who committed the terrible act. It is his to live with now, not mine—I am free.

My disordered eating is far from being completely gone, but it is so much better than it has ever been. Releasing the burden of the emotional trauma of sexual assault, and working through the trauma from my second husband, has helped significantly.

I still struggle with negative self-talk, doubt, and the times when I feel more vulnerable but I am taking on a new outlook, each day practicing CS Lewis' words, "*We are what we believe we are.*" And so, with this mantra and a breath of fresh air, I step out into the world a stronger and happier woman.

I am a strong believer that the universe doesn't give you more than you can handle. I have gone through my life's experiences for a reason, even though I may not yet know the purpose. I am a stronger and more empathic person because of my own pain and struggles.

I hope and pray that my daughters will never have to experience the pain I have gone through, but I know that even with the best of intentions as a parent, I can't always protect them from everything. I am at least grateful that I now have this knowledge to help guide them through life.

My beautiful husband came into my life, and my children's lives, at a time when we were full of trauma from my second husband. He embraced all three of us with open arms, even though we were broken. He was beautifully normal. Not abusive. Not an alcoholic. Not a gambler.

I still remember vividly the day my daughter said to him, "Thank you for being normal and not an alcoholic." This broke my heart and guilt ravished me, but that is for another story. He has taught us to learn to trust again, to laugh and be carefree.

I have never seen my children so alive and happy. This is pure joy. His love and care has helped us all heal. Daily, he reminds me in so many ways that I am beautiful, I am loved, I am sexy, and I am worth loving.

Finally coming back home to my authentic self, I am discovering that the scared little child who existed in me for so long is no longer my driving force. Now, I am a strong capable woman who is slowly releasing her attachment to trauma and self-betrayal, and is becoming emotionally available to her own Self, and to others.

I have finally broken the spell, and in letting go of the pattern of betrayal, *I choose myself.*

II

WHEN A DOOR CLOSES, A WINDOW MAY OPEN

NINA ABBOTT

I SUPPOSE EVERYONE HAS been betrayed at least once. The first time, you feel this annoying disturbance inside of you that tries to deny what is happening. This then becomes like a void that returns every time you are betrayed. Afterwards, you can feel inclined to avoid any circumstance that could be potentially dangerous. Betrayal is simply an experience that never gets easier.

The only thing you can hope to gain is the wisdom to deal with it in a more effective way, rather than not to deal with it at all and keep making the same mistakes. I have found myself doing this at times, but I try to be aware so I don't fall into this trap. I prefer to look at the open window, rather than the closed door.

Despite the fact that it can be blurry, somehow I have kept the memory of my first betrayal experience deep in my mind. School can be an amazing place for some people but, for others, that is not the case. Regretfully, the second category is the one that applies to me.

As a child, when we learn about the world and live in a protected environment, we don't yet have the tools to deal with this kind of experience. I suppose this was also difficult for my parents to grasp because they were not able to help me. Both of them had been popular at school so they could not really understand what I was going through.

Later in life, I learned that the person who set everything in motion had a deep jealousy of what, for me, was a given: the love and attention of an amazing father. I realized then that I was luckier than she would ever be, and this recognition allowed me to set this experience aside and live my life under my own terms.

It is, of course, easier said than done, because I did not want to play by anyone's rules and there are people who can feel threatened by that. When you become someone who cannot be controlled or manipulated, you have to be crushed.

The anger I felt then for being attacked because I did not want to yield to this dominant girl, made me think about what to do with that emotion and the energy that went with it. That energy could help me destroy but it could also help me create, so I decided to align myself with the second option. In time, this decision formed a part of my identity and became the fuel and motor to keep me going, even when things were tough.

You are one decision away from either ruining your life or building something that can help you move forward. Choosing to move forward doesn't mean that everything will be perfect, but it does prevent you from being caught in a negative spiral that can be hard to escape.

After this school experience, my life perspective changed. It made me immediately distrust people instead of giving them a chance. Years later, after participating in a coaching program where a lot of life experiences were shared and discussed, I realized that I was holding myself back from the possibility of establishing interesting connections with others, and limiting the creation of new life experiences in the process.

Creating New Life Experiences

This creation begins with your dreams, so that when you get the opportunity to make them true, you will pursue them. Since I can recall, I have always wanted to discover the world through words. So I flew away into other universes where I could choose to be a spectator or a participant of the story.

When I read, I feel an instant connection with the story, like it is playing a movie in my mind. Our creation center, what we also call our *inner self*, can always help to face the world and provide guidance. It is the place I go to look for answers when I need them.

This place can also be linked with my intuition, which has been present within me since my early years. Unfortunately, I have not always paid it the attention it deserves; if I had, it may have saved me some trouble along the way. It is something I have decided to keep in mind when making decisions, especially if they involve something like the story I am going to share with you. There are always lessons to be learned. It doesn't matter what age you are.

I was young when I started to work and, even though it was not the path I truly desired, I tried to make the best of it. I always knew that my passion lay in the meaningful stories I read and saw on films, and in the end, that road led me to what I wanted to try: working with words.

The Betrayal

In January 2022, I met an editor through the internet while looking for interesting projects on a freelancer platform that I check once in a while. There it was: a post asking proofreaders for help. They needed people to give their opinion regarding the readability of a manuscript.

Something already told me that the task would probably not be paid because there was no mention of that at all, but I was curious to see what it entailed. So I wrote back to ask for more information about the work and whether it was going to be paid.

In answer, I was informed that it was "free of charge but could lead to future opportunities." I was also told that this was a start-up publishing company exclusively focused on the online market and, therefore, environmentally friendly. Even though I love paper books, I found this an appealing approach. It could also be risky, but I wanted to find out where it could lead so I decided to give it a try.

The language combinations I work with are Dutch to Spanish and English to Spanish, so I received the Spanish text to proofread. Honestly, I was surprised to discover that this version was already on sale. This fact alone should have warned me not to go ahead.

I discovered that the manuscript was full of mistakes, from the proper way to write a sentence that is understandable and easy to read, to punctuation and conjugation of verb tenses. In order to publish a book, it first has to be proofread and edited. You are selling a product to customers who are paying for something that is supposed to be finished. Nevertheless, I wanted to believe that this could be a good chance for something interesting, so I ignored my own inner warning.

When I submitted my feedback about the manuscript, the editor asked me if I would be interested in translating the text into Dutch by saying, "I am not actively looking for someone, but if you are up to the task you can do it. As payment, you will get 20 percent copyright of the sales."

I answered that I was willing to try but not on my own. I would need a translation partner to work with me. I wanted to be sure that the quality of the text would be like one of a native speaker and I did not feel confident enough to do the work without help. This meant finding someone who would also accept that kind of deal. My proposal was accepted and I began to look for a partner who was prepared to share this risk with me.

It was not easy to find someone. I totally get it; people are reluctant to jump into the unknown and take such a risk. So I approached a couple of classmates from my translation school—who found the risk too big or not a match for them—and also some people who were recommended to me.

Everyone said no. One of them was pretty rude, acting as if I was trying to mislead him while I had explained very clearly and openly about the type of project and the risks it could involve.

I was beginning to lose hope of finding someone to work with, so I decided to approach the situation differently. I realized I should propose this to someone who could invest their time without taking other risks and, with that in mind, I resumed my search and found a work partner.

The next step of the process was the contract negotiation, which was also not an easy task. There were not only issues regarding the conditions if something went wrong, but also with the deadline, and the typos in it represented another problem.

Looking back, this was an additional sign that something was not working as it should. An editor should be able to deliver impeccable work, especially in a legal document. In the end, the issues were resolved and we were able to start the translation.

Since this was not the first book I had worked on, I knew that it was better to work as fast as possible because unforeseen situations can always arise.

A few weeks later, a post on *LinkedIn* suddenly drew my attention. A new author, a mother of several children, had recently published a book about her last-born daughter—a child who was *different*. I found her story so inspiring that I decided to write to her to ask if she would be open to the possibility of a translation for her book into English and Spanish. She wrote back to tell me that she was certainly open to an eventual collaboration; the only thing I needed to do was find someone willing to publish the translated versions.

The editor I had been working for came to mind, so I wrote to ask if this was something we could do together. After some hesitation, because the book did not fit in with what the publishing company was working on at the time, I received a positive answer. The rest of the email explained what I should propose to the author, including the details I should negotiate for myself.

We outlined the project via some more email contact, and planned an e-meeting for the editor and author to meet each other and further discuss the project. The editor then told me that I would be kept informed about everything that would be decided and carried out after that meeting, but that did not happen.

At that time, I was already busy working on the first book translation and other projects. The initial manuscript had an uncommon topic, which meant that there were challenges to be solved in order to translate it properly. I was caught up in this and my other work, and time went by without me noticing.

I do realize it was foolish not to closely monitor what was going on, but I somehow thought that because all that was discussed and agreed was written down, it was also going to be respected.

As I did not receive any updates, I did what I normally do in this kind of annoying situation: I took action. It is never worth the time and energy to keep pining about something if you can get to the truth of it instead. In my opinion, it is better to go straight to the source and ask directly what you want to know. So I sent the author an email to ask what had happened about her book translation.

The answer I received was entirely unexpected; the translation had already been done by two other translators and was only waiting to refine some details before being published. The author also mentioned she was feeling impatient because the editor had not given any updates regarding the publication and marketing of this version—something she had expected to be arranged a while ago. I thought to myself that she was experiencing the same thing she had done to me, but recognized that she did not realize this. In the last sentence of the email, I was told that they would continue with their plan because of the increasing demand for the Dutch and English versions of the book. And that was it.

I was astonished and it took me a moment to process what I had just read. The first thing that came into my mind was how heartless people can sometimes be, and how quickly professionalism and work ethic are forgotten when it becomes convenient.

The second was that she did not know that I was the brain behind the marketing strategy—a plan that neither she nor the editor would ever be able to use.

I have rarely been as furious as I felt during the next three days. I tried to keep this to myself, but I was too angry to do so. Sometimes it can be helpful to ask someone you trust for their point of view, as it will probably be more objective than yours at that moment, so I asked my youngest brother what he thought. He told me what I already knew, "Take the time to think it through before you take action. Don't rush things you can regret." It was not wise to make a decision under those circumstances.

On the third day, after I had the chance to think things through, I emailed the editor to expose the facts as written by the author and ask for an explanation. The answer I received was simply outrageous, "Ok, I have to talk with... before we decide about the next step. The English version is the priority before working on anything else." No guts to acknowledge the mistake, explain it, apologize, or show remorse.

As I read this, I thought about the possible actions I could take. I explored the potential of starting a legal process using the emails as evidence, but the risk of being involved in a long, tiring, time-consuming, and expensive process did not seem very appealing.

I was also wrapping up the other project with my translation partner and was not in the mood to lose any more of my time in an untrustworthy work relationship, and keep her involuntarily involved in something she did not know. That's why I decided to explain to her what had happened, and inform her that I was not planning to invest more of my time in that project.

She understood my point of view and gave me her support. Later, I heard that the author of the manuscript had decided to pull the plug on the project, so all our time and effort may never see the light. It seems that people can be right when they say, "You get what you give."

The Unexpected

In the end, I decided to give the situation some time to unfold, because you never know when life can surprise you. Not long after I made that decision, I was approached by Tracey, one of the founders of this amazing collective of women, who asked if I would be interested in sharing my story with other women. Suddenly I remembered my childhood dream, when I fantasized about the idea of becoming an author—but was too introverted to think it could ever become a reality.

But here I am, writing. Something good can also flourish from something bad. It simply depends on the perspective you use to assess each situation.

Not long ago, I heard a podcast from Tony Robbins who explained that, "the Chinese word for crisis is composed of two characters: one of them represents danger and the other one represents opportunity." Apparently, it depends on how you look at a crisis to determine the result you will get. Interesting, don't you think?

It is funny how time and a *closed door* can change everything around you. There is a point in life where you are capable of turning around your perspective and seeing things differently, just like this setback has turned out to be a chance to show me another option. There is no point in hanging out in the past because you can't change it.

This *window* guided me here and revealed something amazing, something I was not expecting. Time is the only thing that is really *ours* in life, and it is up to us how we use it, so think intentionally about how you are going to use yours.

FITTING IN AND FALLING OUT

TRACEY BROWN

I STRUGGLED A LOT with female friendships growing up. For most of my life, I assumed it was caused by the simple fact that my father worked in the airline industry and we moved around from state to state. This meant that I was always 'the new girl,' desperately trying to learn the new lingo, trends, and social hierarchy in order to fit into well-established social groups.

I constantly felt like I was missing some secret ingredient to being cool, fun, well-liked, and popular. Don't get me wrong, I was liked well enough—but I was never one of the 'cool kids' and I always felt out of place.

While I'm sure that relocating every two-to-three years was certainly a contributing factor, what I've come to understand as I've become a 'woman of a certain age' is that the feelings of isolation, exclusion, judgement, and insecurity are also deeply ingrained wounds that many—if not all—women struggle with as a result of the patriarchal structures of our society.

The more I've explored the concept of the 'sister wound,' the more I see the patterns of betrayal that are woven into the fabric of our society and our individual experiences, and the more certain I am that the time has come for women to shift the story for ourselves and for our daughters, nieces, granddaughters, and all the women who will come after us.

The first experience of betrayal I can recall dates back to my days in kindergarten when my best friend accused me of being "not nice in nature" simply because it turned out my beloved Cabbage Patch doll was a fake. I hadn't known, and I was devastated. I don't recall ever seeing or playing with that doll again, and the following Christmas, a brand new, genuine Cabbage Patch Kid found its way under the Christmas tree.

What is it that makes five-year-old girls so bitchy to each other? How do so many of us learn these behaviours so early in life? These patterns of behaviour, the clique formations, the exclusions, and gatekeeping when it comes to friendship start early in our childhoods and ingrain themselves deep in our subconscious so that we don't even realise we're following the patterns in the first place.

Frenemies Forever

As I moved through my school years, these patterns continued to come up in my friendships, albeit in different ways that only now am I noticing are symptomatic of the same origins.

The women in my maternal line, from my mother and her younger sister, back to my grandmother and her sister, had attended the same all-girls boarding school. I grew up knowing that even as we moved around the country, I too was destined to attend when I hit high school—no matter where my parents were stationed at the time. So when I reached the Eighth Grade and my family was based on the other side of the country, off I went to boarding school.

One of the girls I was good friends with during that first year of boarding school seemed to 'dump me' as a friend once another girl joined our dorm halfway through the year, and the girls who were in my form class were not girls I'd formed strong friendships with or even had anything in common with. Another friend, a girl in the year above me, unexpectedly and vehemently rejected my friendship with no explanation, which left me confused and feeling like I'd done something wrong; I just couldn't work out what it was. Even though I was now living with all these other girls, I felt like I was *still* on the outside looking in, the odd one out, the weird and uncool girl who never managed to find her place.

And yet, despite this, I can't say I didn't have a fairly large circle of 'friends'—I just wasn't besties with any one person in particular, which was something I desperately longed for. I was looking for that one person who was *my* bestie, and I was theirs.

Throughout all those years of moving around, a pattern continually plagued me: every time I changed schools, I had to break into established friendship dynamics and was often the third wheel in a friendship. After a while, the two original 'besties' always seemed to end up leaving me out and going off on their own. It was the same in boarding school, both in the boarding house and during school hours. I still felt lonely, isolated, and like I didn't belong even though I had a large group of friends and could 'fit in anywhere.'

To be honest, I can't even count the number of betrayals I experienced—and contributed to—during those high school years.

In the Ninth Grade, I recall being hauled into the Vice Principal's office because of a letter I'd written to one of the girls in my year who had a go at me because I was dating her ex. The letter was spitefully written and I was so proud of myself for taking her down a peg or two—until I was pulled up for it and made to apologise. I don't know that putting two teenage girls in a room and forcing them to apologise to each other has ever brought about an authentic and heartfelt apology, or mended rifts, but we both went through the expected motions. And for the record: the boy in question wasn't worth the trouble—but I'm sure even if I could go back and try to explain that to my fourteen-year-old self, it would fall on deaf ears!

In the Tenth Grade, my parents moved back to Perth, and I formed a close bond with a girl in my year who appeared bright and bubbly and lived close to my new home. She was skilled at ingratiating herself into social groups while using humor to mask her manipulative and catty nature. I'm a fairly 'roll with it' kind of person, so I let her take the lead in our social activities outside school.

She had a crush on a guy, who had previously dated her best friend. In order to keep him in her social circle once her bestie dumped him, she set me up on a blind date with him, in the strange and twisted hope that he would notice her while she extricated herself from her own relationship. Unaware of her ulterior motives, I discovered her plan when he rejected her advances and, much to her annoyance, expressed genuine interest in me instead.

Without going into all the details of teenage drama, our friendship became a competition. She was jealous and expected me to conform to her wishes, while I struggled with feeling unsafe and insecure. I had to balance my desire to fit in with the crowd against my urge to stand up for my beliefs and boundaries.

More than once, she attempted to set me up with someone to remove me as an obstacle in pursuing her own romantic interests. Another time she even kissed my boyfriend, expecting him to leave me for her. She also resorted to spreading lies about me within a mutual friendship group, to cause conflicts and misunderstandings when I dared to nurture friendships that didn't include her.

Despite the turmoil and drama, our friendship ultimately led me to meet the man who would later become my husband and the father of my children. The joy of witnessing my children grow into independent young adults has brought purpose to my life, and this alone makes all the angst of our teenage friendship worthwhile.

Many other toxic female friendships continued to follow throughout my teen years and into my early twenties, shifting from high school drama to workplace politics. The common thread seems to be when I've found myself in a dynamic where the relationship has held zero consideration for me, my desires, or my well-being and has been solely focused on how my value, and what I bring to the table, benefit the other person.

The two biggest betrayals I've experienced with this pattern have both occurred in the past five years.

The Mother-in-Law Wound

My former mother-in-law and I used to be incredibly close. I started dating her son when I was eighteen, and during the next twenty or so years we spent over a decade working together and almost a decade living together. We had a good relationship overall, with a few caveats.

She hadn't liked my eldest brother-in-law's previous girlfriend and wasn't afraid to voice her opinions about her. I wasn't particularly bothered by this, but should have recognised it as a warning sign, especially when coupled with the fact that she'd fallen out with her brother and sister-in-law for several years, and her extremely small friendship circle consisted of friends she seemed to fall out with on a a regular basis. Naturally, it was never 'her fault.'

Because I was so young when her son and I got together, and only a few years older when we had our children, it felt like she dictated how I should do almost everything. Clearly, she felt I needed to be told exactly how to be a mother, a wife, and a housekeeper.

Interestingly, this dynamic never existed between my mother-in-law and either of my sisters-in-law. I believe that this is because they were older when they met her sons, and they already had entrenched ideas and beliefs of their own. They held firmly onto these beliefs, even when she disagreed or tried to lecture them on the truth as she saw it. Regardless, she respected them as adults even when they saw things differently from her.

My experience was much different. I came to hate the phrase, "Now Trace, what you ought to do is..." because I learned that whatever she said next was likely to be something I disagreed with, and that I'd have to choose between one of two unpleasant outcomes.

The first outcome was to agree with her, even though I didn't, because it was better for *me* to feel misaligned than face the second outcome. The one where I spoke up, and disagreed with her. Invariably, voicing my opinion led to a belittling lecture that left me feeling like I wished I'd just sucked it up and agreed with her; disagreeing was a thousand times worse.

Despite this dynamic, I loved her, and I was devastated when our relationship came to an end in early 2018. We'd been living with her since 2012 when she'd convinced my husband that the family home was too big for only her and that it needed a family living in it.

Although we'd been together for twelve years, we'd barely been married for a year and I distinctly recall telling my husband before we moved in that it would be the biggest mistake we would ever make. He assured me that it would only be for twelve-to-eighteen months, and yet there we still were, six years later when we ultimately ended up deciding to relocate overseas.

She was so difficult to deal with that he never actually stepped up to tell her we were moving. He knew how she would react. I didn't want to be the one to tell her either, because I knew that her reaction was a shit show waiting to happen, and to be honest, I was afraid of becoming collateral damage.

In the end, she found out, but not because I told her directly. And not even because I consciously intended for her to find out—although in hindsight, I almost certainly subconsciously manifested the outcome.

One of her few close friends was a woman we both knew through a local farmers' market where we'd been selling my mother-in-law's products for several years. Worried about how my mother-in-law would cope once we were gone, I shared my concerns with her friend one morning at the farmers' market and asked her to look after my mother-in-law once we left.

I don't know what I was thinking, or why it didn't occur to me that the first thing she'd do would be to run straight to my mother-in-law and tell her—because that's exactly what happened. And yes, it turned into exactly the shit show I'd been afraid of.

Just as she had done twelve years earlier, when we'd mentioned the possibility of moving interstate, my mother-in-law launched into a negative propaganda and emotional blackmail campaign. She dredged up every possible story of people who'd moved to Italy and lost their money, got divorced, or were attacked by terrorists at Christmas Markets, all while also telling us that we were tearing the family apart and taking away her reason for living.

She even asked why we couldn't wait until she died before we moved overseas, because surely we knew she wasn't going to live much longer and it wasn't unreasonable for us to wait. For reference, she was only sixty-nine at the time, and as I write this five years later, she's still in marvellous health considering her *advanced age* and all.

It only took ten days of listening to this litany of tear-filled emotional pressure before I cracked and told her it was too much, that bearing the weight of being someone's reason for living was too heavy, and that it was unfair of her to put that on us (especially when she'd spent most of my husband's childhood moving around as an expat wife).

She never said another word about it to me, but whenever I wasn't home she redoubled her efforts against her son, convinced that it was solely *my* idea to move to Italy and that he was just humouring me. To this day, she still believes this to be true, and my ex has never once told her that, in fact, he was as much, if not more of, a driving force in the decision to up and relocate.

This was only the first schism in what ultimately destroyed our relationship beyond repair and it was only three months later when the second, most catastrophic schism occurred. In the days leading up to it, we'd finally booked our airline tickets, and our departure date became set in stone. Once again, my husband failed to tell his mother and the responsibility fell on my shoulders. I spent three anxiety-ridden days trying to work out how I was going to approach her.

She took it surprisingly well when I finally found the words, or so I thought.

The thing about sharing a house with someone is that it's very hard to have private conversations when you leave doors wide open, which is something my mother-in-law did often. Her bedroom was separated from the kitchen/meals area by an adjoining narrow hallway, and she almost never closed either the hall or bedroom doors while also spending most of her evenings lying in bed chatting on the phone for all to hear.

On this particular day, my then-ten-year-old daughter and I were in the kitchen preparing to go shopping. I hadn't been paying attention to the sounds of conversation coming from my mother-in-law's room until I heard my name. Then, clear as a bell, I heard her completely tear me to shreds as she spoke on the phone.

I didn't actually care about most of the things she said, from questioning my intelligence and my understanding of the way the world works, to completely ludicrous and untrue versions of conversations we'd shared... but when she started ripping into my sister (who had also worked for her, as a favour, on and off for years) and my parents (who had never been anything but supportive of her, including looking after my kids every weekend while I attended farmers markets with her *for years*), I saw red.

I couldn't bear the thought that my daughter, who stood there in the kitchen, was being exposed to her vitriol. The idea that my daughter's feelings about her auntie and grandparents could be influenced by her words left me feeling sick with rage. Somehow, I managed to calmly walk over to her bedroom door and very quietly say, "I'll thank you not to talk about my family."

My mother-in-law reared back like a cut snake, dropped the phone, and screamed at me to "Get the fuck out of my room," because I shouldn't have been "standing at her door eavesdropping."

Shaken, I walked away and headed back into the kitchen where I asked my daughter if she was ready to go, and we headed off to meet her Scout patrol group at the supermarket to shop for their camp supplies. I don't remember what I told my husband when I got home, or how he reacted, but as far as I was concerned she'd crossed a line she couldn't come back from.

For the next two-and-a-half months we didn't speak a word to each other. She made no attempt to apologise, although I did hear her on the phone to my sister-in-law about a month or so later, as she walked through the house, telling her that she "was going to apologise, but she's got such a fucking attitude, that one," which I found hilariously funny even as it continued to fuel my rage. For my part, I'd been acting as if she didn't exist, which was clearly making her feel *something*.

Two weeks before we left she approached me to apologise and, naive fool that I was, I believed she was genuine and agreed that we could try to build a bridge in our relationship. Two days later, my sister-in-law, niece, and nephew flew in to stay with us for the weekend to say their goodbyes to the kids, and we all played 'happy families.'

It felt like old times, and I thought it was a new beginning for us all, but as soon as my sister-in-law flew out, it was like I'd dreamt the whole thing. My mother-in-law reverted to being a heinous bitch and doubled down to make our last week and a half absolute hell. The final time we drove away from that house, the night before we flew out, I couldn't help thinking how *fucking glad* I was that we were leaving the country and would never come back to that house again.

Moving to Italy was like a balm to my soul, and the freedom that came with the almost complete break from my mother-in-law changed all our lives.

Even though my husband and I ended up separating at the beginning of 2023, one of the things we both still agree on is that the decision to move to Italy and put half a world between us and his mother was one of the best decisions we ever made.

It was like a giant weight had been lifted, and the skies had finally cleared after years of being stuck in the centre of her storm. We all flourished, healed, explored, and made friends and connections in our new home. Some of the women who form the circle of my closest female friends were made in those pre-pandemic days in Italy. It was magnificent, and I was constantly filled with joy, love, gratitude, and abundance.

Experiences Offer Unexpected Gifts

I'd launched my online business just as the pandemic hit, but I was lucky enough to connect and collaborate with some incredible women who helped me through those dark days of isolation. As I leaned into the power of the feminine, I found my soul sisters, my voice, and my message. But as I continued to up-level my personal growth, I experienced a new layer of betrayal to unravel.

In mid-2021, I wrote my first chapter in a bestselling book, and as a result of the skills I brought to the table during and after the launch, my publisher asked me to do some freelance work for her. We'd become friends and it wouldn't be inaccurate to say that I was just as invested in the success of her business as she was.

I went above and beyond the scope of the work she was paying me to do because I felt deeply connected with her vision for the books she wanted to create. We envisioned and brainstormed ideas daily. Anything that was in my power to deliver, I attempted to create for her, and in return, she made me *feel* like I was her partner, her right hand, indispensable.

Except that I wasn't.

She asked me to create a publishing support proposal for her, to put into writing all the things I could do, and price them in a way that "lit me up" and would make me "want to jump out of bed in the morning." It took me a while to get my act together because being asked to value my own worth brought up a surprising number of blocks for me, despite being intimately familiar with money mindset and shadow work.

Eventually, I sent her my beautifully crafted proposal, which had been tailored especially to her needs. She told me how great it was and that I'd even be able to use it to offer my services to other indie publishers!

And this is where it all started to go wrong because that's exactly what I did. She'd explicitly given me her permission, and yet when she discovered that I'd not only pitched my services to an emerging publisher—none other than my *Aligned Leaders* co-author, and now partner, Jenny—and been chosen over her own pitch (which I didn't know about at the time, but ironically would have still been mostly me delivering white-labelled services!) that our relationship changed permanently.

No longer did she message me daily and tell me how much she appreciated me or my work. We entered a toxic cycle of stonewalling, gaslighting, and love-bombing.

Our messenger chat went from, "I appreciate your help. I hope you had an amazing day yesterday and a prosperous day today! Good night! Love you so much," to, "I would love to get your feedback on this. Thanks."

At first, the gaslighting made me question whether I was imagining the whole thing. So I messaged her to ask if I'd done something to upset her. "No! I love you!!" She replied. And then more silence, punctuated only by my unanswered attempts to reassure her that I was still fully committed to her publishing house and her infrequent, impersonal, generic messages that left me feeling like she was deliberately shutting me out.

I was heartbroken and this situation triggered a lot of unresolved feelings from my fall out with my then-mother-in-law. Fears of love being taken away, of losing someone important in my life, of being made to feel like it was my fault for doing something unacceptable and audacious. *Who was I to dream of something bigger than what was being offered to me?*

Most of the time, I simply felt heartsick, despite having so much to look forward to.

While all this was going on, the idea for my *Lunar Wisdom* book come flooding in, and I spent an entire day mapping it out, from the women I wanted to call in, to the reasons why I wanted to write and publish this book, and why at this moment. This too caused me anxiety, because, on top of working with another publishing house, I'd have to tell her that I was going to launch my own book—through my own publishing house, not hers.

This gave me flashbacks of having to tell my mother-in-law we had booked our tickets to Italy. I was afraid that speaking to my publisher would play out exactly the same way, forming an irreparable rift that I did not want at all. In truth, my reasons for not publishing through her publishing house were simple and had nothing to do with her as a person.

I had decided to pay my authors royalties, and I knew this didn't fit her business model. It was the one thing I couldn't compromise on, and it meant that I was going to have to publish it under my own banner. And so *Gemini Moon Press* was born.

Even though I was struggling with the shift in that relationship, I was lucky that I now had Jenny to bounce my ideas off. She loved some of the 'disruptive' and 'audacious' ideas I wanted to try out with *Lunar Wisdom* and suggested we also try them with her book, *Quiet and Badass*. It was so refreshing to have someone who not only saw the possibilities in my vision for what I desired to create, but who also aligned with them.

Jenny also opened my eyes to just how toxic the dynamic was in my relationship with my publisher—it was hard to see the wood for the trees in the middle of the emotional turmoil—and she kept reminding me that there was nothing wrong with wanting to create something of my own, and doing it in a way that felt fully in alignment with my own values and vision.

Inevitably, the situation with my publisher did end up playing out more or less the same way I'd expected, although there was never a big confrontation as there had been with my mother-in-law. Surprisingly though, despite a couple of months of angst as I detoxed from the love-bombing and gaslighting cycle, letting go of that relationship ended up being a lot easier and less painful than I'd feared. It fizzled out quietly, and we slowly ended up walking our separate paths.

We both still work in publishing but we have very different visions of the kinds of books we want to create within the industry and the authors we want to work with—and that's okay because there's room for both of us to do our own thing and we very rarely cross each other's paths.

The amount of healing, growth, transformation, and abundance that I've achieved and received as a result of that relationship falling away is incredible. My betrayal experiences also brought me the freedom to pursue my own dreams, and I can't even begin to articulate the depths of my gratitude for the women who stepped up to write in *Lunar Wisdom* with me, who saw and felt my vision for that book and said YES!

Publishing *Lunar Wisdom* showed me just how deeply passionate I am about not just publishing books that *matter*, but also how strongly I feel about helping other women to share their stories, knowledge, wisdom and power. To then have the opportunity to follow on with *Betrayed* and the *Wounded Women Series*, with Jenny and our incredible authors by my side is simply beyond words.

If you take nothing else from these stories, know that there is truth in the belief that despite how much pain, frustration, anger, hurt, and every other emotion that bubbles up within you in the heartbreak of betrayal—whether it's a betrayal of self, betrayal from another, or your own betrayal of another—if you're willing to do the shadow work, break the cycle, and look for the silver linings, you'll see that there really are opportunities for healing, growth, abundance, and purpose waiting for you to seize and make the most of them.

If we can do it, you can too.

MEET THE AUTHORS

JENNY ALBERTI

Jenny Alberti is Co-founder of the Women Writing Intentionally Collective, the CEO of Introvert She Wrote Publishing, a Content Marketing Coach, and an International Best-Selling Author. Through her multiple roles that empower women and promote self-expression, she is dedicated to helping female visionaries share their stories, earn recognition for their talents, and fulfill their dreams of becoming published authors.

Through her uniquely designed book projects and programs, Jenny's mission is to powerfully amplify the voices of all women who aspire to create an epic impact on the world. She firmly believes that embracing our true selves and our uniqueness is crucial for personal and professional fulfillment. She inspires her authors to break free from societal expectations, authentically express themselves, and fearlessly share their valuable messages with the world.

As a self-identified introvert, Jenny initially found the nature of online entrepreneurship overwhelming. However, she embraced her personality and capitalized on her innate talent for written communication, which helped her successfully navigate the noisy online landscape.

In 2021, she achieved her childhood dream of becoming a published author. Jenny is living proof that introversion, social anxiety, and fears of visibility can be transformed into inspiration, momentum, and the fuel to create lasting change. Her expertise and accomplishments as a writer and disruptor in the publishing industry have garnered international recognition, with features in *Authority Magazine* and an invitation to become a Senior Executive Contributor to *Brainz Magazine*.

Despite her strong roots in Northern California, where she resides with her loving partner and cherished fur-babies, Jenny nurtures her love for travel and adventure through seeking inspiration around the world. In her downtime, she takes great pleasure in immersing herself in the pages of captivating horror novels.

TRACEY BROWN

Tracey Brown is co-founder of the Women Writing Intentionally Collective, the CEO of Gemini Moon Press, a Certified Moonologer™ and Lunar Business Strategist. It was Tracey's love of working with the moon that led her to write her first chapter in a collaborative book project in 2021, making her an international best-selling author.

With a deep-rooted passion for empowering spiritual women and amplifying their voices, Tracey is dedicated to the sharing of Divine Feminine and Sacred Ancestral wisdom.

Under her publishing imprints, Tracey creates safe and nurturing spaces for women to speak their truth, share their wisdom, and heal the wounds of the past. She firmly believes that their narratives deserve to be heard, celebrated, and cherished, as they carry within them the essence of ancient wisdom that can guide and inspire us in the modern world and lay the foundation for collective healing. Her book projects are curated to encourage collaboration and opportunities for women to step into their power and authority.

As a respected writer and speaker, Tracey's expertise has been featured on renowned platforms such as *Thrive Global*, *Elephant Journal*, *Medium*, and various podcasts, including Yasmin Boland's *Mainly Moonology* podcast. Her insights into the intertwining of natural rhythms, ancestral knowledge, and inner wisdom have resonated with audiences worldwide.

Tracey's book, *Lunar Wisdom: Reconnecting with the Divine Feminine through Rituals, Spells, Magic, and the Phases of the Moon*, provides inspiration and guidance from fourteen diverse lunar women, showcasing various practices that encourage readers to create their own personalized and aligned lunar practice.

Although an Aussie girl at heart, Tracey currently splits her time between sunny Northern California and beautiful Northern Italy. She adores her partner, children, and fur fam. When she's not immersed in her work, you can find Tracey reading, enjoying the outdoors, exploring the world, or taking leisurely walks with her Bengal cat, Maple.

TERI KATZENBERGER

Teri Katzenberger is the CEO-Founder of the Live Well Now Academy LLC and has been a Fitness, Nutrition, and Weight Management Specialist since 2000. She is an "incredible overcomer," a divine woman who has a passion for all people from all walks of life.

As a young adult, Teri became the survivor of a traumatic domestic violent marriage, a lifetime of disabling self-image issues, a chronic health-altering eating disorder, and a chronic life-threatening alcohol and drug addiction. To save her own life, in 1991 Teri began her own personal health and wellness journey. Since then, she has dedicated herself to helping and teaching people how to live a healthy, well, fit, strong, and whole life, from the inside out.

Her dedication, passion, and life experiences make Teri the perfect choice for those who want to stop the diet "roller coaster" and embrace sustainable changes, while learning to feel great about themselves. More and more, people today want to live a full, healthy, and happy life; Teri combines her education and desire to help people look and feel great about themselves.

As a Personal Life Coach and Accountability Partner, Teri works with her clients through 1:1 Sessions and Group Coaching, both globally and in person. Her specialty lies in helping people to achieve their best life as she guides and walks alongside them throughout their journey of transformation. Teri teaches and shares hard truths to help people achieve real and lasting results.

Teri is an international best-selling author with features in publications such as *Authority Magazine*. She holds a diploma as a Fitness and Nutrition Specialist from Penn Foster University, and has a Medical Fitness Certification Specialization in Menopause Hormone Fitness, along with numerous other certifications.

Her Mission Statement is: "To educate and train people in Fitness, Nutrition and Weight Management and to enhance their lifestyle physically, emotionally, and spiritually."

RUTH FAE

Founder of Fae Blood Publications, Ruth Fae is an Intuitive Writing Coach and Editor, International Bestselling Author, Speaker, Youth Mentor, and Chief Editor at the Women Writing Intentionally Collective. A believer in the unlimited potential of co-creation, she helps silenced voices be healed and heard through the powerful, timeless, and magical process of storytelling.

Through her years as a journalist and copywriter, Ruth learned that sharing the wisdom of our experiences helps us to heal, nurture, and create true connection. In a non-judgmental space, and by working with the energy and guidance of the Lunar Cycles, she guides aspiring and established authors to align with their inner magic and sacred truth, find their voice, and release shame and doubt. Through Ruth's transformative guidance, her clients step into inspiration, confidence, and authentic expression.

A rebel at heart, she loves to challenge convention through working with publishers and authors within the world of Indie Publishing. As an avid lover of the performing arts, and with a keen interest in encouraging the voice of our younger generations, Ruth values her years of experience as a columnist, reviewer, and editor for Dance Writer Australia and Indigo magazine.

More recently, she has shared her stories about life, writing, and the power of communication in four diverse collaborative books—*Lunar Wisdom*, *Magnetic Abundance*, *Get Published*, and *Navigation Tools to Thrive in the Human Experience*. She can also be found on Medium, and loves to explore the many facets of writing, editing, parenting, transformation, and spirituality as a podcast guest.

Residing in Melbourne, Australia, Ruth Fae shares her 'Life of Love and Magic' with her partner, their blended family of seven children, and an adorably naughty puppy named Merlin.

NINA ABBOTT

Nina Abbott is a Chilean Translator and Editor living in The Netherlands since 2001. An avid reader from a young age, Nina has always dreamed and created stories in her imagination. After finishing high school, she studied a quick secretarial course and started working just after that.

Her love for literature and words remained alive, but asleep, until an unexpected change of plans created the possibility to pursue a career in the translation business. She has worked for Saga Egmont Publishers, BroadStreet Publishing, and in the translation of the bestselling book, *Corporate Rehab: Ditch the Hustle Culture and Thrive Again*. She has also performed subtitling for the Dutch TV channels VPRO and BNN Vara.

Nina is participating in *Betrayed*, because she hopes that her story inspires other women to follow their dreams and find their inner strength, even if they find themselves in a difficult situation.

AMANDA NORR

 Amanda B Norr is a Certified Moonologer™, Healer, Intuitive, and International #1 Best-Selling Author. Her mission is to connect with and guide others to find healing and Divine connection through working with the Moon.

Amanda's card readings combine a unique blend of intuition and coaching that helps her clients unlock, integrate, and embody the divine guidance they receive. She also loves to work with herbs, oils, and crystals. Her first book, *Lunar Wisdom,* was published in 2022, and she is thrilled to be a contributing author in all three *Wounded Women Series* titles, *Betrayed, Broken,* and *Burned*.

Now a proud grandmother of two, Amanda has spent the past twenty-six years living on a dairy farm and raising two children with her husband. After selling their cows in May 2023, she is leaning into agriculture in a new way. Amanda also supports her local community as a volunteer EMT and Firefighter, and loves to read, write, and crochet.

CHRISTINE FREY

Christine Frey is a Shaman and Reiki Master Teacher and Practitioner who owns Centerpoint Healing Services, in Colorado Springs, Colorado. She is a wife and mother with two adult sons and a daughter-in-law. Christine is passionate about helping people feel valued, heard, respected and not alone as she works in-person and around the world.

A survivor of 49 years of domestic violence, sexual assault, incest and human trafficking, Christine is boldly empowered to help people with her 33 years of training in trauma, Reiki, yoga and Shamanism.

She contributed to the best-selling book, *Quiet and Badass*, and has recently been accepted into the top 50 of *Who's Who In America*, having received many nominations for her role in helping erase prejudicial stigmas, helping people find their authentic voice and her volunteer work helping survivors in her community.

LINSEY JOY

Linsey Joy is an Intuitive, Law of Attraction Coach, and International Best-Selling Author. She has been working with Angels, energy, and manifestation since 2009 when she experienced a series of metaphysical events that opened up her world. Linsey helps spiritual seekers ready to see their challenges in a new way, to tune into their own intuition and divine connection for guidance and joy.

Using her intuitive gifts, personal development training, and healing quantum frequencies, Linsey guides clients to shift their limiting beliefs into empowering perspectives and intentions. A former Montessori teacher, she also loves sharing Peace Education curriculums and mindfulness to children, teens, and young adults.

Linsey is a passionate speaker, appearing in interviews and podcasts across the globe. First published at age eight, her multi-author books *Divinity Speaks*, *Betrayed*, and *Burned* are best-sellers. She is a California native, devoted wife, fur-baby mama, gamer, and artist.

STEPHANIE MOYER

 Stephanie Moyer is an Intuitive Empath, Eclectic Witch, and CEO, Founder and Curator of The Conjuring Moon—a Full Moon subscription box service and online Metaphysical shop. One of the thirteen authors of the international bestselling book, *Lunar Wisdom*, her vision is to provide a safe, non-judgmental space for divine feminine warriors to explore, develop, and harness their own unique spiritual practices while helping them break free from societal norms.

Through her own healing journey and spiritual awakening, her goal is to one day open a healing center for all women to help them on their own healing journey through meditation sessions, kundalini yoga, Reiki sessions and trauma therapy.

Stephanie lives in Pennsylvania with her husband, three daughters, grandchildren, and two dogs. When she is not curating boxes or participating in Spiritual and Holistic Expos, she loves to visit Salem, MA, and go to various music fests with her family.

WELLA LILES

 Wella Liles is the woman behind wellasworld.com where she writes about mom-life, relationships, self-care, and the importance of living a life true to yourself. She believes her purpose is to live life to the fullest while helping others in any way she can, from holding doors open to guiding them to heal from their past experiences so they can be more present with their family and meaningful work.

Her articles have been featured in *Inspiring Lives Magazine* and *Thrive Global*.

When she's not writing, she's either running errands with her husband, running after her little ones, or snoozing on the couch while watching Netflix shows.

TERESA FOX

Teresa Fox is a Nurse, Mother, Writer, and Founder of Foxy Holistic Wellness, where she empowers others to step into who they truly are and uncover their most authentic version of Self.

An addictive behaviour and mental health clinician with a background in trauma-informed practices, Teresa is a multi-modality energy healer, retreat facilitator, and course creator who combines her love of positive mental health with holistic practices. Teresa supports people on their transformational journey to step with wonder into self-discovery and activate authentic change in all areas of their lives.

Teresa's idea of a perfect day begins with an ocean swim with the "cold water crazy girls," followed by a cup of tea, energy healing, meditation, and writing in her journal, which has led to her current literary endeavour as she steps into the power of her voice through becoming an author.

"Awareness flows from the spirit on the journey to empowerment."

Teresa Fox

HELEN STAINES

 Helen Staines is a Business Entrepreneur, Youth Mentor, and Quiet Philanthropist. A believer in nurturing our youth, she and Jamie, her husband and Coffee Staines co-founder, create a family-like environment with positive employment opportunities that the kids can take into their future careers.

Coffee Staines' mission is to provide a broad menu for all people, regardless of their dietary requirements. Their unique café, event, and wedding catering allows everyone to enjoy a diverse and safe culinary experience with their loved ones and friends.

During her fifteen years in Corporate Management, Helen has managed distribution centres across Australia, navigated multi-million-dollar contracts, and nurtured hundreds of staff. She brings a wealth of experience to both business and people management, and loves nothing more than to help others grow to their highest potential.

Helen believes that every business can create change and make a difference. Her desire for connection and philanthropy has led her to become highly involved in her community. She finds great joy in making a difference to someone's day!

Residing in Beechworth, Australia, Helen is blessed to share her passion for business, growth, and life with Jamie, their blended family of three children, and their spoiled and much adored Alaskan Malamute, Koda.

DISCOVER THE

WOUNDED WOMEN SERIES

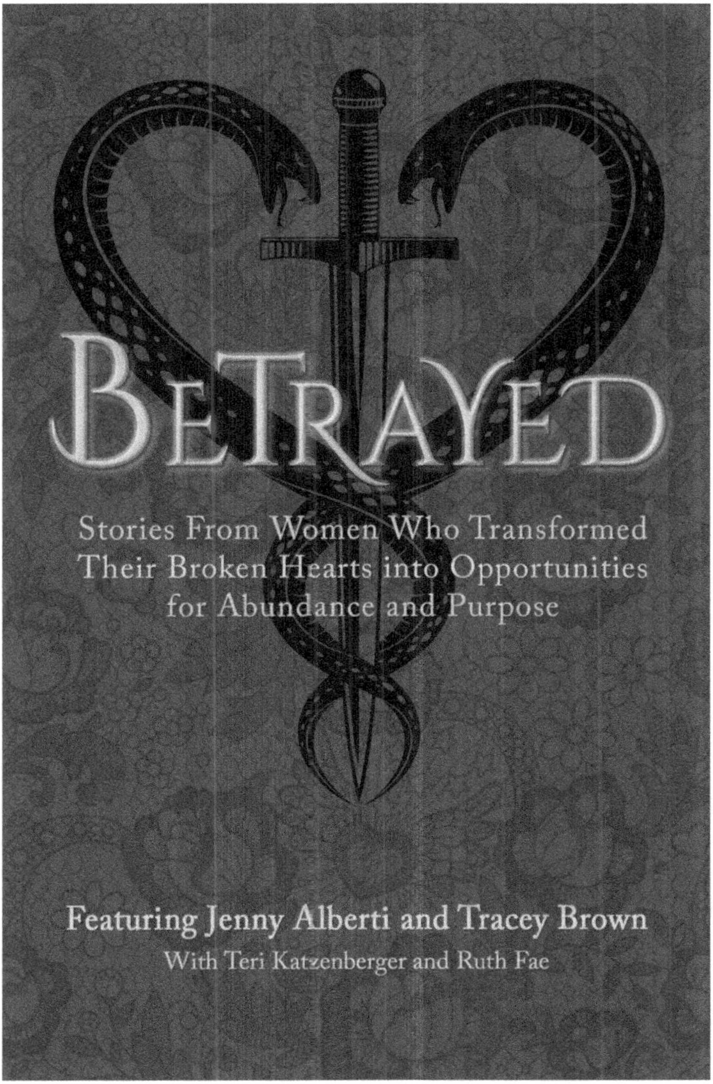

BETRAYED

Stories From Women Who Transformed
Their Broken Hearts into Opportunities
for Abundance and Purpose

Featuring Jenny Alberti and Tracey Brown

With Teri Katzenberger and Ruth Fae

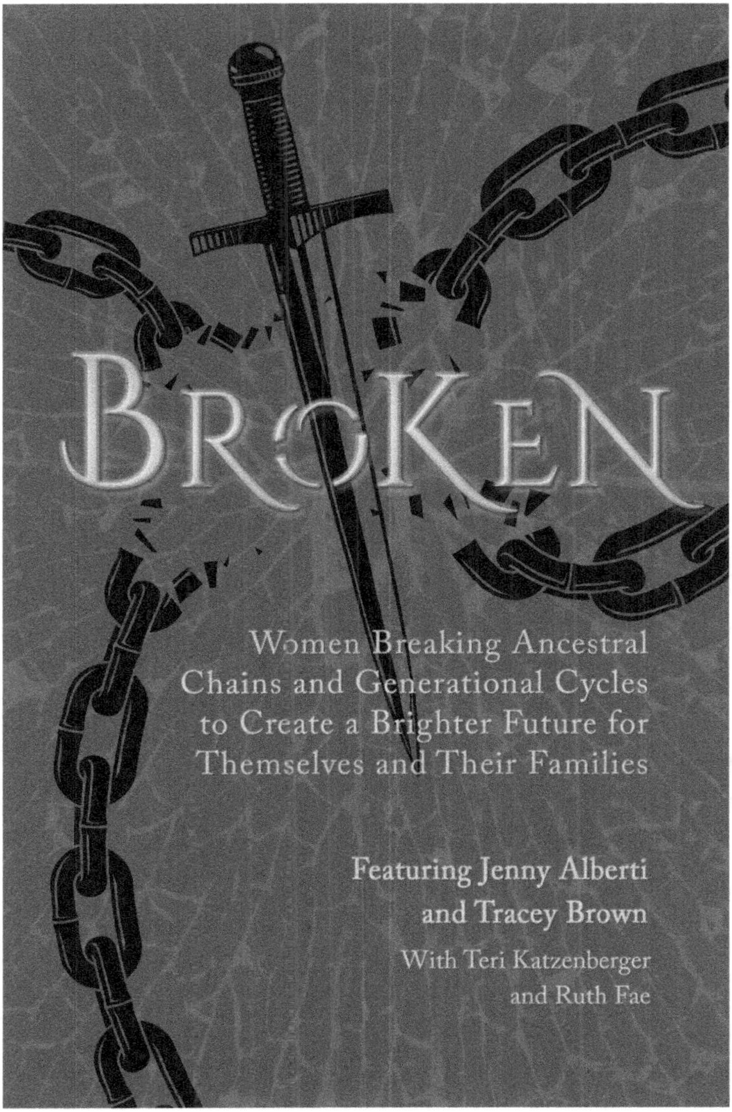

BROKEN

Women Breaking Ancestral
Chains and Generational Cycles
to Create a Brighter Future for
Themselves and Their Families

Featuring Jenny Alberti
and Tracey Brown

With Teri Katzenberger
and Ruth Fae

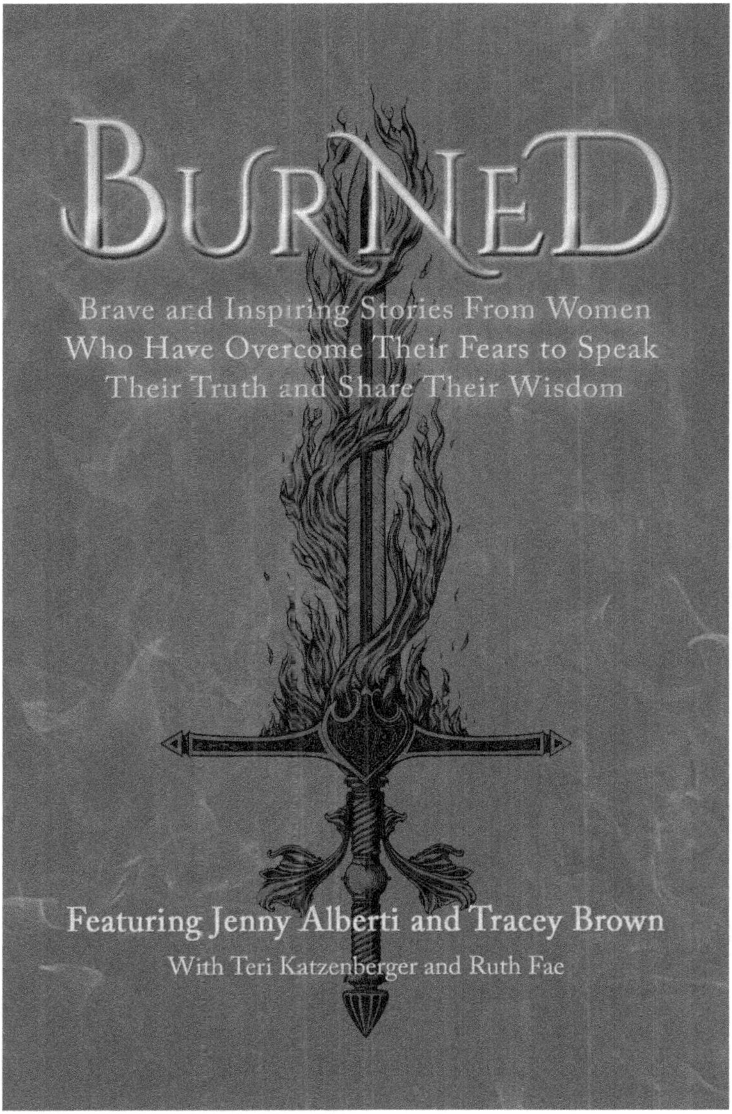

BurNeD

Brave and Inspiring Stories From Women
Who Have Overcome Their Fears to Speak
Their Truth and Share Their Wisdom

Featuring Jenny Alberti and Tracey Brown

With Teri Katzenberger and Ruth Fae